BLACK SABBATH

BLACK SABBATH

SABBATH

SONG BY SONG

STEVE PILKINGTON

FONTHILL

Fonthill Media Language Policy

Fonthill Media publishes in the international English language market. One language edition is published worldwide. As there are minor differences in spelling and presentation, especially with regard to American English and British English, a policy is necessary to define which form of English to use. The Fonthill Policy is to use the form of English native to the author. Steve Pilkington was born and educated in England; therefore British English has been adopted in this publication.

Fonthill Media Limited
Fonthill Media LLC
www.fonthillmedia.com
office@fonthillmedia.com

First published in the United Kingdom and the United States of America 2018

British Library Cataloguing in Publication Data:
A catalogue record for this book is available from the British Library

Copyright © Steve Pilkington 2018

ISBN 978-1-78155-661-0

Typeset in 11pt on 13pt Sabon
Printed and bound in England

CONTENTS

Introduction

Few people would argue that Black Sabbath defined the idea of what heavy metal music represented in people's minds in the 1970s, and even after the advent of such genre-changers as thrash, death metal, progressive metal, etc., from the 1980s onward, Sabbath are still acknowledged as 'founding fathers'. Indeed, while the likes of Cream (via 'Sunshine of Your Love'), The MC5 (via 'Kick Out the Jams'), and even The Kinks (via 'You Really Got Me') have all variously been credited with 'inventing' the 'metal' genre, there can be little doubt that Black Sabbath were the first to distil that vague recipe into the finished article. However, when the original, and to most people, definitive, line-up of Ozzy Osbourne, Tony Iommi, Geezer Butler, and Bill Ward first came together, it was in a six-piece band with the unlikely, and uninspiring, name of the Polka Tulk Blues Band. The origins of the name are disputed, with various parties remembering it differently as coming from either a brand of cheap talcum powder or a Birmingham clothes shop. In any case, the name was soon shortened to the scarcely better Polka Tulk, before the four future Sabbath men decided they wanted to continue as a four-piece, without the other two members (slide guitarist Jimmy Phillips and sax player Alan Clarke), but, seeking to avoid the unpleasant confrontation of sacking the pair, they split the band before quietly reforming as a four-piece under the name Earth.

Around this time, Tony Iommi, ironically on his last afternoon of work, suffered the factory accident that famously severed two of the fingertips on his right hand (and, as a left-handed player, therefore his fret hand). When he became determined to still play, after being inspired by jazz guitarist Django Reinhardt (himself missing two fingers), he fashioned plastic 'thimbles' for the missing fingertips by melting and shaping the plastic from a washing up liquid bottle. Nowadays, of course, they are made for him, but he still uses thimbles based on exactly the same design almost fifty years later.

During 1969, when playing under the Earth name, they had started to become heavier and louder—supposedly so that people would be unable to ignore them—and had survived Iommi's very brief defection to Jethro Tull (with whom he would appear in The Rolling Stones *Rock and Roll Circus* film), when it became clear that another band with the name Earth was causing some confusion. They adopted the name 'Black Sabbath' from the current popularity of horror films and novels. *Black Sabbath* was the title of a 1963 horror film, and though the band maintain that they had not seen the film in question, a 'black sabbath' ceremony described in a Dennis Wheatley novel led to the writing of the song of the same name. Soon after this, they adopted Black Sabbath as their name, and were on the road to becoming the stuff of legend.

The original foursome remained together until 1979, with one brief hiatus when Ozzy left in 1977 to be replaced briefly by ex-Savoy Brown singer Dave Walker. This short-lived line-up made one TV appearance on a BBC programme entitled *Look Here* in 1978, performing 'War Pigs' and an early incarnation of 'Junior's Eyes' with different lyrics. After Ozzy returned later that year, the band recorded the *Never Say Die* album and embarked on a tenth-anniversary tour before parting company with the increasingly erratic Osbourne again, this time seemingly for good.

The second 'great' phase of the band arrived in 1980 when Ronnie James Dio, recently departed from Rainbow, joined the band for the massively successful *Heaven and Hell* album, with some fans swearing that this line-up was the best the band ever had. Again, it was relatively brief, however, with Dio leaving after one more album (and a live album), and the band's career began to become more fragmented. With Bill Ward having himself departed after the first leg of the *Heaven and Hell* tour, the next couple of decades saw the band going through a variety of members, with even the loyal

Butler eventually leaving Iommi as the sole constant member, while singers such as Ian Gillan, Glenn Hughes, Ray Gillen, and, with the most stability, Tony Martin passed through the ranks; there was even another stint with Dio. The late '90s saw an improbable reunion of the original line-up, which led to an on-off career through to the present day, although Iommi and Butler did at one stage reunite with Dio and drummer Vinnie Appice under the name Heaven and Hell, named for legal reasons after the album they most famously represented—although, confusingly, Bill Ward had played on the album itself. The last, and seemingly final, album recorded by the original four was the 2013 album called, fittingly, *13*. This book will take us through the whole of this fascinating career, by way of a look at every single song and album released by the band along the way—hopefully proving as much of a journey of (re)discovery for the reader as it did for the author.

1

Black Sabbath

Release date: 13 February 1970 (note: this was a Friday). The album
                was not released in the US until 1 June 1970.
Record Label: Vertigo (Europe), Warner Brothers (US)
Personnel: Ozzy Osbourne, Tony Iommi, Geezer Butler, Bill Ward

The album was produced by Rodger Bain, who also went on to
produce albums by Judas Priest and Budgie. The whole thing was
recorded in one day, in October 1969, over a twelve-hour period,
then mixed on the second day. The album went into the UK charts on
the first week of release, eventually climbing to No. 8—an astonishing
achievement for a band who had received almost no coverage in the
music papers before its release, based almost wholly on 'word of
mouth' reputation. Ozzy Osbourne remembers taking a copy home
and playing it for his father, who was supportive, but baffled. 'He
turned white as a sheet,' recounts Ozzy, in his autobiography *This Is
Ozzy*, 'he rubbed his eyes and shook his head. He didn't get it at all.'
The album later went on to reach No. 23 in the US.

   The sinister photograph that adorns the album sleeve was taken at
Mapledurham Watermill in Oxfordshire. The identity of the woman
in the photo has been lost, though Tony Iommi has claimed that she
once turned up backstage at a show and introduced herself. The
inner gatefold featured an inverted cross with a gloomy poem inside.
Originally white on a black background, this was later reversed to
black on white.

Songs

'Black Sabbath'

Written by the band as an attempt to convey a horror film in musical form, the band actually named themselves after the song. They were still called Earth when the song was written, but seeing the popularity of it, they changed their name and refined their musical direction overnight. The title was coined by lyricist Geezer Butler after he read the book *The Devil Rides Out* by Dennis Wheatley, in which a 'Black Sabbath' ceremony is described (there was a 1963 Boris Karloff film named *Black Sabbath*, but the band insist none of them were aware of it at the time). Butler claims to have seen the 'black shape' referenced in the song at the foot of his bed, at a time when he was obsessed with the occult, and had his flat painted black and decorated with inverted crosses; he claims that he was so scared by the incident that he abandoned his fascination with the subject immediately. He has stated that Ozzy had given him a book about the occult, which had unnerved him to the extent that he hid it in his airing cupboard, and that after the shape appeared, he ran to the cupboard only to find the book gone. Whatever the truth of this, he redecorated the flat immediately and steered clear of any practical magic involvement.

The song itself has been described as the template for the heavy metal genre, and it is ushered in by the sound of rain and a tolling bell before Iommi's crushingly heavy slow tritone riff comes crashing in. Ozzy's vocals brilliantly evoke the nightmarish scene of the protagonist losing his soul to Satan, while the song continues through a fast midsection and into a galloping, irresistible coda, which comes to a shuddering halt, leaving the listener breathless. Indeed, this is an example of how Ozzy, despite not being a technically accomplished singer, was absolutely central to Sabbath's sound. His anguished cry of 'Oh no, no, please God help me!' in particular is masterful. A musical genre was born here, and the song was to remain in the band's set list through all of their line-up changes until the end of their career.

An early radio session recording of the song was included on Ozzy's compilation album *The Ozzman Cometh* in 1997, featuring a rare third verse before the up-tempo section. For the record, this cheerful addition runs 'Child cries out for his mother/Mother's screaming in the fire/Satan points at me again/Opens the door to push me in'. It is not an essential version, to be honest, and inferior in every way to the album track.

'The Wizard'

An unusual song in the Black Sabbath repertoire as it features the central riff played on harmonica by Ozzy. The inspiration behind the character of the wizard himself, spreading joy as he goes, has been long debated. Rumour has it that it was actually referencing a drug dealer with whom the band did business, and it has also been suggested that it was inspired by the Tolkien character Gandalf. However, Iommi has claimed in his book *Iron Man* that the idea was born from an incident when Osbourne and Butler were walking around somewhat stoned and saw someone outside a club acting bizarrely, and they imagined him as the character. The song is more upbeat in feel than most of the album, being a bluesy number representative of the material the band were performing when they went under the name Earth. It was later released in 1970 as the B-side of the massive hit single 'Paranoid', which led to it becoming somewhat better known.

'Behind the Wall of Sleep'

Another insistently heavy track, this one eschews any attempt at a chorus or leavening of the music in any way, being an oppressive delivery of another unnerving, if surreal, lyric. Allegedly inspired by the H. P. Lovecraft story *Beyond the Wall of Sleep* (not unlikely given the well-read Butler), it has little connection to the story beyond the theme of visions communicated through sleep. Others have interpreted the references to 'deadly petals with strange power' and suchlike as referring to opium. Whatever the inspiration, it is an impressively eerie listen, if not an obvious popular standout—which made it all the more surprising when the band reintroduced it to their live set recently after an absence of over forty years. The US edition of the album credited the introduction to the song with the separate title 'Wasp'—it clearly refers to the first thirty seconds, after which the song's central refrain enters, but in actuality, it was a method of gaining increased publishing royalties via more song titles. The same tactic is used in two more places on the album.

'N.I.B.'

Probably the most debated song title in the band's history, 'N.I.B.' was long speculated to stand for 'Nativity in Black', until it was claimed by Butler that they had no title for the song and in the end simply named it after the pointed shape of Bill Ward's beard at the time, which was reminiscent of a pen nib. The title was made into initials simply to make it more mysterious. It is easy to see how the assumption was made, as the subject matter of the lyric concerns a young woman falling in love with Satan, written from the point of view of the smitten Dark Lord in the first person. Ah, romance! The song is a no-holds-barred riff-driven stormer of a track, which remained a live favourite throughout the years, driven by a riff that takes its basis from Cream's 'Sunshine of Your Love', but develops it into a circular, insistent motif that drives the song along propulsively and unstoppably. Once again, Ozzy proves the trump card here as his triumphant cry of 'Oh yeah!' midway through the riff each time it comes along is a brilliantly catchy hook. It makes little sense in the context of the lyric, yet it is hard to imagine the riff without this interjection. Indeed, even trying to imagine it without that makes one's mind unconsciously add the 'Oh yeah!' Such was the genius of much of Sabbath's early work—they have described themselves as being like 'a bunch of idiot savants' at the time, making stuff that was extremely successful without really knowing why. One suspects that this is somewhat self-effacing, but it is easy to see what they were getting at: they were young and totally inexperienced studio-wise, but they were creating music that, while superficially quite straightforward, was utterly timeless.

Once again, the US edition of the album listed an extra track here: Butler's short wah-wah bass solo at the beginning of the track is listed separately as 'Bassically' (indeed, this and the previous track are sequenced together as 'Wasp'/'Behind the Wall of Sleep'/'Bassically'/'N.I.B.'). This intro was clearly recorded in one take with the rest of the song, as a close listen reveals the sound of Butler's bass being audibly turned up before he goes into the riff.

'Evil Woman'

The first of two cover songs on the album, this one was included at the behest of the record company, who were anxious for something a little more commercial to be included as a possible single release.

It was released as a single in some countries, with non-album track 'Wicked World' on the B-side, but it failed to chart. The song was originally performed by a Minneapolis-based band named Crow, included on their 1968 debut album *Crow Music*. Sabbath's version follows much the same arrangement, but is unsurprisingly heavier, with the original Crow version relying very much on a horn section (which was reportedly added against the wishes of the band in any case). It is a catchy song, and fairly punchy in the hands of Iommi's power chords, but relatively insubstantial. The song was omitted from the US pressing of the album in favour of its B-side, 'Wicked World' (see p. 16).

'Sleeping Village'

'Sleeping Village' is an odd song. Beginning with a softly played acoustic guitar, accompanied by a lazily picked Jew's harp (uncredited, but supposedly played by producer Rodger Bain), the lyric consists of a mere four lines. Ostensibly describing a peaceful scene as the village in question awakes one morning, the opening 'Red sun rising in the sky' suggests the possibility of some disaster about to befall the unfortunate villagers, but this is all open to interpretation. To be honest, given the band's lyrical preferences at the time, impending doom is a pretty safe bet. After less than a minute, Iommi's energetic, upbeat guitar figure ushers in the whole band and jolts the listener out of the torpid atmosphere. Over the course of the next three minutes, this jaunty riff breaks down into a far more doomy section, punctuated by some frantic drum fills from Ward, which appears to presage the track 'War Pigs' from the following album. A double-tracked guitar solo then takes us into a reprise of the doomy part before segueing directly into the following track. It is interesting, but unusually constructed. It seems to suggest that the instrumental section is perhaps playing out the events suggested by the opening vocal part, and certainly conjures up ideas in the head of the listener.

Once again, this track has a separately credited opening on the US release, credited as 'A Bit of Finger'/'Sleeping Village'/'Warning'.

'Warning'

The final song on the album, and listed as a separate track on the European pressing, unlike the US version, it nonetheless segues directly from the end of 'Sleeping Village', with a slightly bluesy guitar riff opening up the track. Another cover version, this time the song is written by legendary drummer Aynsley Dunbar, who played with Frank Zappa, David Bowie, and Lou Reed before going on to perhaps his most high-profile position as drummer on the first four Journey albums before later stints with Whitesnake and UFO, among others. 'Warning' was originally performed by his own band, The Aynsley Dunbar Retaliation, released as a single in 1967, after he was fired by John Mayall. The Dunbar original is quite weighty for the time, but a little pedestrian, and the song is completely revitalised by the extraordinary treatment given to it by Sabbath. Ozzy takes the lyric and twists and turns it into an incredible cry of anguish, giving lines such as 'the sea began to shiver and the wind began to moan' a complete new life. This hugely dramatic reading of the song is then taken to another level by Iommi's lengthy improvised soloing, over the running time of ten and a half minutes. A six-minute instrumental jam section provides the centrepiece before we are taken back to Ozzy's final declamation of the final verse and chorus. A perfect closer to the album, it begged the listener to flip it back over to side one and that rain and tolling bell, and play the whole thing again.

Notably, this album marked the first and last time that Black Sabbath would include covers of other people's material on their albums. Iommi was becoming more prolific at churning out riff after riff, and the band's self-penned material began to pour forth.

Related Song

'Wicked World'
One further change in the American pressing of the album saw 'Evil Woman' being replaced by another original composition, 'Wicked World', which was unheard by many UK listeners until it was finally released on the double compilation album *We Sold Our Soul for Rock 'n' Roll* in 1976. It had appeared on the B-side of the 'Evil Woman' single, but few had heard that. The song had been performed live by the band in the intervening years, as evidenced by its appearance on the belated live release *Live at Last*, recorded in the mid-1970s, but not released until the early 1980s.

It is in fact quite a strong piece, and there is a convincing argument that it deserved its place on the album. It is undeniably heavy, yet displays an almost jazzy sense of swing courtesy of Iommi and Ward especially. The lyric, while clumsy in places, delivers a still-potent message lamenting mankind's ills in the form of war, disease, and poverty within its fairly concise three verses. An early indicator that, even at this point in their career, Black Sabbath possessed a social conscience, which was often overlooked completely amid the satanic imagery. This lyrical vein would be more and more fully explored over the next few albums.

2

Paranoid

Release date: 18 September 1970. The album was not released in the
US until 7 January 1971 due to the fact that the debut
album was still in the charts when the UK release date
came about.

Record Label: Vertigo (Europe), Warner Brothers (US)

Personnel: Ozzy Osbourne, Tony Iommi, Geezer Butler, Bill Ward

Like its predecessor, the album was again produced by Rodger Bain.
Recording took place over a six-day spell from 16–21 June 1970, a
veritable age in comparison to the single day it took the band to blast
through the previous album. It reached No. 1 in the UK album charts
(the only Sabbath album to do so until *13* repeated the feat in 2013, an
astonishing forty-three years later). In the US, the album reached No. 12.

The front and back of the gatefold sleeve feature an oddly dressed
warrior, complete with sash, appearing in blurred form from behind
a tree in darkness, brandishing a wickedly curved sword. If the image
appears completely at odds with the title, that is because the record
company elected to change the title of the album from the intended
'*War Pigs*' to '*Paranoid*' at the last moment, but decided not to change
the sleeve design. The official line was that they feared the title '*War
Pigs*' would cause controversy with the then-high profile Vietnam War
coverage, but many, including Osbourne, insist that it was far more
to do with the 'Paranoid' single riding high in the charts. The inside
gatefold contains a shot of the band atop a grassy ridge. Osbourne is

standing apart from the rest, but this was apparently a doctoring of the original photo in order to fill up the gatefold and fit the text in between. Butler is credited as Terry 'Geezer' Butler—the last time he would be listed using his real first name on a Sabbath record.

Songs

'War Pigs'

Opening the album with a slow, doomy, sparse riff, this is clearly taking its album-opening cue from the debut, but the resemblance ends there. Right from the word go, it is clear how the band have progressed even in a few short months since the first album, as Butler's bass perfectly counterbalances Iommi's funereal guitar chords by effectively supplying the opening melody. Howling sirens loom from the sonic hell to enhance the air of heavy business in every form before the song abruptly changes tempo, with Iommi's simple yet effective two-chord figure upping the ante on the proverbial dime. According to Butler, this was created spontaneously from a jam in the song 'Warning' one night, when Iommi suddenly hit that double chord and they knew they had something right away. This section of the song is filled out in superlative fashion by Bill Ward's drum pattern, showcasing for the first time how much his almost jazzy, unconventional style was to bring to the band.

The song was originally written with the title 'Walpurgis', from the pagan (and in some accounts, of satanic origin) festival widely celebrated in mainland Europe, but this was rejected by the record company as being too satanic-sounding, and potentially off-putting. The band agreed to rechristen it as 'War Pigs', but no words needed to be altered as they were already complete in the recorded form. A defiantly anti-war song, Butler remembers it as having been specifically against the Vietnam conflict, but Ozzy refutes this, claiming that none of them knew enough about Vietnam and that it was a general anti-war sentiment.

The lyrics open with an oft-ridiculed couplet, as Butler rhymes 'Generals gathered in their masses' with 'Just like witches at black masses', but he was to comment years later that he simply could not think of an alternate rhyming word and that it 'wasn't a poetry competition anyway'. Ozzy is in strident form as he declaims the lines in commanding form, accompanied only by Ward's skittering rhythm, before once again proving how vital he was to those early recordings by signing off the end of each verse with a heartfelt 'Oh lord, yeah!'. Again, like the 'Oh yeah!' in 'N.I.B.', it is simply impossible to imagine the track without this interjection now. Try to sing it without it—it cannot be done!

Over the course of its eight-minute duration, the song moves from this original verse pattern through a churning midsection, back to the first verse template again, before finally going into a closing instrumental section that is deceptively intricate. A brisk, speeded up tape conclusion wraps things up dramatically and unexpectedly, providing a quite breathless end to one of the most enduring of all Sabbath songs, and probably the most enduring track on the album. Note that, as with the debut, the closing section of the song is separately titled as 'Luke's Wall', but again, this is only present on the US release.

Like the version of 'Black Sabbath' described earlier, a radio session recording of the track from April 1970, still titled 'Walpurgis' and with different lyrics at the time, was included on Ozzy's 1997 *The Ozzman Cometh* compilation. In this incarnation, the infamous opening couplet is replaced by 'Witches gather at black masses/Bodies burning in red ashes'—it is easy to see the different lyrical slant matching the 'Walpurgis' title. This is a very interesting track to seek out, actually.

'Paranoid'

Ah yes, 'Paranoid'. The Sabbath song that everyone knows, fan or not. Their own 'Smoke on the Water', 'My Generation', or 'Stairway to Heaven', if you will. The freak Top 5 UK hit single that came out of absolutely nowhere (and was never followed up, naturally). Yet the strange thing is that the song was written as a throwaway piece to fill up some time, and was the last, quickly recorded, thing to make the album. According to the band, they were asked to come up with 'a short song' to make up the time, and on returning from the pub to the studio, Iommi picked up his guitar and started playing the intro riff. The other guys scrambled for their instruments, and as they claim now, 'within about 20 minutes or so', the whole song was basically sketched out. Indeed, audio does exist of a formative take with Ozzy seemingly making up words on the spot just to get the vocal melody in place—though they include some references to the finished song's themes of people imagining the central character is mad, and the influence of a woman on his condition, the finalised lyric was completed by Butler, influenced by encounters and experiences he had had with paranoia and depression. For all its throwaway nature and commercial success, it is still a very powerful and heavy song, with a lyric that is as far from the typical chart fare of the time as you could imagine. Again, that is Black Sabbath all over—even when they crashed the party of the mainstream singles chart, they did so on their own terms and in an almost subversive way.

'Planet Caravan'

A complete departure from the rest of the material on either of the first two albums, this dreamlike track nevertheless heralded a run of albums on which Sabbath would feature at least one acoustic ballad or instrumental. Iommi himself admits to doubts at the time about whether the track should go on the album, but it was deemed to be a successful experiment and went on to enjoy some popularity. Accompanied by Ward's hand drums, Iommi's acoustic guitar playing on the track is heavily influenced by legendary Belgian guitarist Django Reinhart, whose playing, despite the handicap of two paralysed fingers on his left (fretboard) hand, was a massive inspiration to Iommi following his own accident in which he severed his fingertips. The track also features piano, which was played by engineer Tom Allom. Geezer Butler describes the lyrics as a kind of outer-space romantic love story, with the protagonists sailing past the moon and through the solar system on a kind of ultimate romantic weekend, with the bassist commenting on the *Classic Albums* TV programme that he 'wanted a change from the "let's go down the pub and have a bag of chips" kind of thing'. Ozzy's otherworldly sounding vocal with its trebly vibrato effect was achieved by him singing directly through a Leslie speaker, and Rodger Bain then using an oscillator—memorably described years later by Ozzy as looking like 'a fridge with knobs on'.

'Iron Man'

While it is probably fair to say now that the song's impact has been blunted by over-familiarity and audience-participation driven live renditions, there is no denying the fact that 'Iron Man' was an important, and iconic, song in the early Black Sabbath catalogue. Butler's lyrics, when looked into closely, are astonishingly imaginative, as the song tells a story that is more involved than many might think, laced with heavy irony. It concerns a scientist who develops a time machine that he uses to go forward to a time when he witnesses an apocalyptic future in which mankind meets its violent demise. While travelling back to warn the world of this fate, and urge them to take steps to avoid it, he is involved in an accident involving a magnetic field, which turns him to steel, leaving him unable to communicate the vital message he has to impart. Hurt, frustrated, and enraged by the way his attempts to communicate are ridiculed and dismissed, he ultimately embarks on a vengeance-fuelled rampage of destruction, becoming the very instrument of mankind's destruction from which he had sought to save them. It is an immensely powerful and symbolic storyline, which was surely missed by many a casual listener.

Musically, the song is driven by a relentlessly simplistic repetitive riff, which found an enormously receptive audience among the legions of people eager to absorb the burgeoning heavy rock movement. It was a time in which heavy bands were seemingly sprouting up like mushrooms, but it is uncertain whether the term 'heavy metal', despite having been immortalised years earlier in the Steppenwolf song 'Born to be Wild', was yet being used routinely to describe the music. Before the lyrics were conceived, the song went by a working title of 'Iron Bloke' when Ozzy, hearing for the first time Iommi's great slabs of distorted power-chording in the introduction, leading into the riff, was moved to comment that 'It sounds like some great iron bloke walking around'. Which, in fairness, it did. As the song develops, it belies its rather basic foundations by utilising some tempo changes that are remarkable in the way the band execute them so perfectly and in such harmony, with the instrumental section towards the end of the track galloping to a thrillingly unstoppable conclusion. Without a doubt, the track was one of the defining moments of early '70s heavy rock music, and an astonishing way to finish the original first side of vinyl.

'Electric Funeral'
In the late 1960s, when Black Sabbath were maturing into their familiar form, the world was an uneasy place, living under the constant perceived threat of nuclear oblivion—from the frankly ludicrous 'what to do in case of nuclear attack' propaganda emanating primarily from the US to the much more serious, and terrifying, brinkmanship of

the Cuban Missile Crisis at the beginning of the decade. With this in mind, Sabbath came up with what was almost a companion piece to 'War Pigs' in 'Electric Funeral'—the general anti-war sentiment of the former replaced by specific, and dramatic, nuclear terror in the latter. Some of the imagery in the song, with Ozzy's menacingly sneering delivery of lines such as 'Radiation, minds decay' or 'Burning globe of obscene fire/Like electric funeral pyre', is chilling in the extreme. The verses of the song are a classic example of Sabbath's trick of having the vocal line, guitar riff, and bass line all doing exactly the same thing, and following each other, to great effect. The impact produced here by this technique is almost claustrophobic in its intensity, and imbues the lyrics with infinitely more power than they could ever have on a printed page. The tempo change into the fast-paced mid-section, however, displays quite the opposite technique, in that it may sound like a simple, fast guitar riff, but a listen to what is going on beneath the surface reveals jazz-influenced playing by Butler and Ward; they are quite brilliant in the way they work in contrast to, yet blend seamlessly with the main riff. It is a way of playing that Cream had mastered years before, and yet Sabbath never received the kudos they deserved for some extremely dextrous and clever playing.

'Hand of Doom'

Another war-derived lyric; Butler has stated that his inspiration for the song was from playing US Army bases in the UK and Germany, where soldiers returning from Vietnam would spend some time before being finally shipped home. He was struck by the fragile mental state that many of these young men had been left in, and witnessed just how many of them had taken to hard drugs, and heroin in particular, to numb the pain and enable them to function. The song begins by addressing this particular issue, with its references to 'Vietnam, napalm', and suchlike, before broadening to encompass a warning to any disaffected youth who found themselves turning to the illicit temptation of hard narcotics to either escape or enhance their own reality. LSD is referenced, along with multiple allusions to needles, etc., leading to, once again, grim images of death. There is little on this album to provide light relief by way of subject matter, but every theme explored has proven, nearly fifty years on, to have lost little of its relevance.

The song begins with a slow, methodical bassline, supplemented by sparse rimshot accompaniment from Ward, as Ozzy intones the lyrics in dismal tones; it then cranks up to a big, slow riff following the same rhythm, and Ozzy now declaiming loudly and dramatically, with huge attendant power, before dropping again for another quiet verse. After settling into this pattern for a while, another trademark tempo change is inevitable, and so it arrives, with what could be taken as a rapid marching feel drawing once more from the military genesis of the song. A very dark, yet enormously powerful track, the one-two effect of this following 'Electric Funeral' to open the side almost bludgeons the listener into a state of submission, both in terms of musical power and lyrical doom. The Sabbath template was becoming more and more set with every passing song.

'Rat Salad'

It has been said that every ground-breaking album is allowed one piece of filler material, and such is the case with 'Rat Salad'. The piece was reportedly born of necessity, when the band had to play such marathon sets in their early days that a forty-five-minute drum solo was incorporated just to fill up the required time. The solo here may, mercifully, be only a minute rather than forty-five, but it is still an insubstantial and inconsequential two and a half minutes—still bulking up time, but this time for a side of vinyl, not a drainingly long set duration. The template here is set very much by Led Zeppelin's 'Moby Dick' on their second album, which had appeared a year before, and had somehow made recorded drum solos much more acceptable than, say, Cream had managed some time earlier with 'Toad'. Like the Zeppelin track, 'Rat Salad' begins with a cursory bit of riffage and meandering Iommi guitar work before Ward comes in with his minute of glory and the band play us out with another fifteen seconds tacked on the end. It is listenable, but not a track many would have high on their list of great Sabbath moments.

'Fairies Wear Boots'

The album closes with this heavy slice of boogie-rock, but it is a song whose final form belies its origins. The title originally came from Ozzy, after the band had an unfortunate encounter with a group of skinheads, when he came up with the derogatory phrase 'Fairies Wear Boots' after the Doc Marten boots the skinhead gangs would habitually wear, and which had been unfortunately employed in kicking the hapless Sabbath guys that particular night. Unusually for the time, the lyrics were written by Ozzy, who, having coined the title, found himself in something of a cul-de-sac as to where the song would go, as a literal account of getting into a fight with some skinheads clearly would not really work as a lyric. As a result, the song developed into a bizarre tale of him seeing a disquieting vision of fairies wearing boots and dancing with a dwarf, when he looked into a window late one night while under a hallucinogenic influence, shall we say. So convinced is he of this disturbing scene that he goes to his doctor, only to be informed that he has 'gone too far', because 'smoking and tripping' is all that he does. It is a light-hearted enough romp on the surface, but once again, it does cast a slightly darker pall on the LSD experience than the shiny, colourful likes of 'Lucy in the Sky with Diamonds' or 'My White Bicycle', or other more conventionally 'psychedelic' songs of the time. When the Beatles took us down to 'Strawberry Fields', we were assured that it would be a carefree place where 'nothing is real' and there is 'nothing to get hung about'. When Sabbath took the same route, they ended up seeing ghastly supernatural visions and being abandoned by the medical profession. Such was a large part of what made the band so special, and struck such a chord with so many disaffected youths, and, indeed, still does.

Musically, the song is again more interesting than a cursory listen would suggest. The track opens with an unusual, long introductory instrumental section, complete with guitar solo, which has little or no connection with the main body of the song that follows, and yet, it strangely works perfectly, despite lacking such traditional niceties as consistency of key or tempo. When the huge central riff does kick into life, it has an unstoppable momentum to it that in a sense presages the irresistible boogie of peak-period Status Quo, yet is not really twelve-bar based as such. Listening to the way the band play the riff, it is striking to hear the incredible swing and groove that Butler and Ward in particular put into it. Totally different to the traditional rock rhythm section, it is another classic example of how, with Sabbath, there was so often much more than the apparent sum of the parts going on when one 'lifted the car bonnet' so to speak, and why so much of their material retains a freshness that so many of their contemporaries now lack.

For the next album, where was there left to go? The answer was heavier, and darker still.

3

Master of Reality

Release date: 21 July 1971
Record Label: Vertigo (Europe), Warner Brothers (US)
Personnel: Ozzy Osbourne, Tony Iommi, Geezer Butler, Bill Ward

In his last work with the band, the album was once again produced by Rodger Bain. This was the point when Tony Iommi took the decision to detune his guitar (and therefore the whole band) by three semitones for certain tracks. This was largely to make playing more comfortable with his artificial fingertips, but it also had the effect of making the band's sound instantly even heavier, thicker, and more doom-laden. Recording took place between February and April 1971, the longest the band had yet taken for an album recording session. It reached No. 5 in the UK album charts and No. 8 in the US.

The cover was the starkest and most basic the band had produced so far, rendered in funereal purple and black and containing only the band and album names on the front, while the reverse featured the band name again, with the lyrics reproduced below. Initial UK copies featured a 'carton' sleeve design, opening with a flap at the top and having the band name in purple and the album title embossed in black-on-black. A poster of the band was also included. Subsequent copies reverted to a flat sleeve design, without poster or the raised embossed letters, and had the album title in grey. The initial US print run misspelled the title as '*Masters of Reality*', and featured four more of those 'extra titles' for parts of songs, in the same way as on the previous albums. Subsequent US pressings corrected the title spelling and did away with all but one of the extra titled sections. There have subsequently been several variants worldwide of the colour scheme, with red, orange, and all purple lettering occasionally being used (including one particularly horrendous multi-coloured monstrosity), but always kept the same basic design.

Songs

'Sweet Leaf'

Another classic Sabbath album-opener, the iconic, rolling thunder riff of 'Sweet Leaf' arrives to the echoing sound of a hacking cough. The song—Geezer's anthem to the delights of the large amounts of marijuana the band had become accustomed to sampling—is the first real indicator of the band's embracing of the rock and roll lifestyle, which would come more to the fore on the following album. The cough is actually Tony Iommi, recorded spontaneously after he took a drag on an enormous joint passed to him by Butler, and it makes for an unforgettable, and startling, opening to the song. The simple and yet anvil-heavy guitar figure that propels the song has become one of Iommi's definitive riffs, and the song itself is an acknowledged classic. The title actually comes from a brand of Irish tobacco called Sweet Leaf.

'After Forever'

An avowed Catholic, Geezer Butler wrote the words to this track partly to refute the band's satanic image, although, explicitly pro-Christian as the lyric may be, it still seemed to elude many who would not or did not want to hear it at the time or to look beyond the music. Indeed, in an ironic twist, despite the unequivocally pious message of the song, the band still managed to get into trouble, with complaints being directed at the (unquestionably classic) line 'Would you like to see the Pope on the end of a rope?', which was taken entirely out of context. The track was released as a single, but its message failed to reach the album-burning naysayers as it failed to chart anywhere. Musically, the song is a mixture of light and shade, with the central motif of the song skipping along in a veritably upbeat fashion, while the riffs underpinning the different vocal sections are much denser and heavier. It is a very entertaining, and significant, song, without quite scaling the heights as a Sabbath classic of the highest order. The intro to the track was credited separately on the US release of the album as 'The Elegy', but, as with the previous albums, not in the UK.

'Embryo'

Scarcely a track in its own right, this is simply a short, unaccompanied guitar piece serving chiefly as an introduction to the following track 'Children of the Grave'. It is an interesting composition, with a medieval-sounding feel to it, but nothing more than that.

'Children of the Grave'

Unquestionably the enduring classic from the album, 'Children of the Grave' illustrates the continuing Sabbath knack of making a song title sound as if it is something from a horror film when in fact the lyric deals with a different topic entirely; far from being about any kind of undead or similar theme, the track is another of Butler's anti-war messages, coupled with his belief in non-violent revolution. The titular 'Children' are in fact marching to take over the world in the name of peace and love and overthrow their warmongering overlords, being doomed only to become Children of the Grave if they fail in this noble undertaking. Naïve and clichéd the lyric may be, but it is flung along with such purpose by the driving propulsive rhythm of the appropriately marching sounding riff that it scarcely matters. The song simply has the rolling power of an unstoppable juggernaut, and has been a fixture in the band's set lists (and Ozzy's solo set as well for many years) ever since it first appeared. Indeed, as the years have progressed, the song has gradually usurped the ever-present encore of 'Paranoid' as the set-closer that the die-hards really want, garnering the most enthusiastic response by some margin. The track ends with some eerie-sounding, echoing music with a repeated whispered voice intoning 'Children of the Grave … Children of the Grave…', which would loop endlessly in the run-off groove on the original vinyl. This outro section was credited on the initial US pressing as 'The Haunting', but this extra title was removed for future pressings. They really were trying it on by now with those extra titles.

'Orchid'

Another solo guitar piece by Iommi, this one-and-a-half-minute acoustic piece is far more than another 'Embryo', however. In fact, despite its brief duration, this is a supremely delicate and beautifully composed piece, with a couple of chord progressions thrown almost casually into the middle, which are brilliantly evocative. The short length of the track may be indicative of Iommi's lack of confidence in including such a piece on a Black Sabbath album; this was because, on the following two albums, he contributed similar pieces in the shape of 'Laguna Sunrise' and 'Fluff', which were longer and more fully developed. A supremely effective side opener, paving the way for another more typical doomy rocker following it.

'Lord of this World'

The grinding riff, which forms the thirty-second introductory passage to this track, was originally given the separate title 'Step Up' on that notorious first US pressing, but in reality, it is very hard to see why. Yes, there is an abrupt change into the song's main riff, but that opening section is repeated again during the track, so a separately titled intro makes very little sense—well, except for that trusty financial sense again, of course. The bedrock riff of the piece, when it comes in, is a surprisingly jaunty affair, with a rapid marching feel that lifts the accompaniment from the excessively heavy and oppressive feel of the opening; this is one of the songs on the album using the detuned guitars, and it shows. Lyrically, this is another piece following the 'After Forever' model, being a basically Christian message couched in black imagery: the 'Lord of this World' of the title is, of course, Satan, also referred to in the album title in a similar way. However, the message is a rebuke towards people turning to Satan in their materialistic self-absorbed lives, summed up in the couplet 'You turn to me in all your worldly greed and pride/But will you turn to me when it's your turn to die?'—in retrospect, it was an incredible tightrope act that the band managed at this time, as most other bands using such lyrical ideas would more than likely have been ridiculed for their Christian ideals, but the Sabbath imagery of the much 'cooler' dark side carried them forward. In effect, they managed to escape the gimmicky feel of exclusively black magic-oriented bands such as Black Widow while also making anti-satanic lyrical ideas seem cool.

Quite the trick. As far as this particular song goes in a musical sense, however, it is probably a little long for the musical ideas to sustain it, and it ultimately emerges as probably the weakest of the album's 'heavy' tracks. Good, but a notch below classic.

'Solitude'

Another departure from the norm here, as the band produce another acoustic song in the vein of 'Planet Caravan' from the previous album, only this time, instead of dreamy cosmic imagery, the theme is a tale of desolation and despair. This is really the Tony Iommi show for the most part as, in addition to multi-tracked acoustic and electric guitar parts, he also contributes some nice flute playing (a legacy of an interest gained during his brief Jethro Tull sojourn). Ozzy's voice here is masterful, and showing just how well he could sing at this time—something he is often not credited with. His voice is low and brooding, with lots of reverb applied, and it almost gives the impression of being inside some sort of mausoleum with the mournful voice echoing out of the walls; the atmosphere conjured up is beautifully maintained throughout the song's five-minute duration. In fact, so unfamiliar does the vocal sound that many over the years have speculated that the voice may not indeed be Ozzy, but instead Bill Ward making his vocal debut, but this is incorrect. This song provided the link between 'Planet Caravan' and the following album's more well-known 'Changes', and is an unfairly neglected piece in its own right. Once again, this shows how Black Sabbath could write their own rulebook, and pretty well get away with it every time.

'Into the Void'

Back to the grinding, detuned bludgeoning for the album's closing track, another idealistic Butler lyric about a band of 'freedom fighters' leaving the earth in a fleet of rockets to find another world free from the pollution and general manmade malaise of this one, so that mankind can make a fresh start on a world 'where freedom waits'. Once again, it is a viewpoint and subject matter that could have ended up filed under the 'hippy-dippy' category in lesser hands, but no such worries here, as this is an absolutely monstrous track. With another gratuitously titled 'intro' on that short-lived US pressing, which was christened 'Deathmask' for no good reason, the sense of propulsion and powerful drive provided by the music, as the opening words 'Rocket engines burning fuel so fast…' come in, gives the track an almost breathless impetus. In fact, after that opening slow, crushing groove, the same driving, insistent riff propels almost the entire song, with only a brief up-tempo mid-section and closing guitar solo to break it up—and yet in spite of that (or even for that very reason, given the subject matter), it works brilliantly, seeming much shorter than its six-minute-plus duration. Longer than 'Lord of this World', for example, it seems the opposite. Iommi has said that, owing to the complex drum patterns required and the difficulty of making the extremely verbose lyrics scan, both Ward and Osbourne had enormous difficulties finally nailing this one. It was time, effort, and frustration well spent, however, as this is a superb close to an album that is simpler in structure for the most part than *Paranoid*, yet in many ways closer to the distilled essence of *Black Sabbath*. As would continue to be the case with the next offering.

4

Volume 4

Release date: 25 September 1972
Record Label: Vertigo (Europe), Warner Brothers (US)
Personnel: Ozzy Osbourne, Tony Iommi, Geezer Butler, Bill Ward

Working without Rodger Bain for the first time, the album was produced by Tony Iommi—the band's then-manager Patrick Meehan gets a co-producer credit, but apparently had little actual input. Recording away from the UK for the first time, the band were holed up in Los Angeles in a big rented house, with recordings taking place in May 1972 at The Record Plant. The writing and recording sessions were accompanied by a veritable blizzard of cocaine, which is referenced in the sleeve dedication to 'The great COKE-Cola company of Los Angeles'. The song 'Snowblind' references this, and, in fact, the album was scheduled to have that title, but the record company overruled this and *Volume 4* was used instead. The album reached No. 8 in the UK charts and No. 13 in the US, slightly down from *Master of Reality* but still creditable.

   One of the band's most iconic cover designs, the front and back covers featured a photo of Ozzy Osbourne on stage with arms aloft in trademark fringed jacket, rendered in monochromatic form in yellow on the front and white on the back, with the album title in white lettering (yellow on the reverse) around the top of the picture. The effect was striking and memorable. For the original vinyl pressings, there was a page glued into the album's gatefold to create a six-page 'booklet', wherein each member had one page to themselves featuring one large photo and one smaller one, showing them in action on stage. The centre spread featured a shot of the whole band, taken from behind, during a show at Birmingham Town Hall.

Songs

'Wheels of Confusion'

One of the strongest opening tracks on any Sabbath album, and an often overlooked classic, it is obvious from the very beginning of 'Wheels of Confusion' that the band are stretching themselves out somewhat, as Toni Iommi's strident guitar theme comes in with magisterial power over a funereal-paced, brutally heavy chord sequence. This morphs into a rolling, unstoppable riff, sounding like great tombstones being slowly pushed down a hillside, and the sound is instantly fuller, bigger, and more inexorably powerful than anything that has gone before. Iommi's idea to produce the album himself certainly appears to have paid dividends because, together with the new recording studio—and possibly the blizzard of cocaine around at the time—there is a feeling of the music both breathing and paradoxically feeling claustrophobic at the same time. When Ozzy comes in declaiming 'Long ago I wandered through my mind…', it is clear that Butler's lyric writing has moved into a somewhat more metaphysical area than his previous subjects, and this all adds to the epic feel that the track, and indeed the album as a whole, exudes. A bleak message dealing with the futility of earthly endeavours unfolds ('The world will still be turning when you're gone'), interspersed with one typically frenetic trademark Sabbath mid-section breaking things up superbly. As the song winds to its apparent conclusion, a suddenly triumphant, celebratory coda emerges, with Iommi soloing over an irresistible, descending chord progression, and via a lengthy fade-out, we are at the end of a marvellous eight-minute statement of intent.

Note: that lengthy climactic section is sometimes given the separate title of 'The Straightener', and when played (infrequently) live, the band would omit this section, probably owing to the amount of overdubbed guitars involved.

'Tomorrow's Dream'

This relatively short three-minute track was plucked from the album for release as a single, but it failed to chart anywhere. Hardly surprising as there is not all that much commercial appeal about the song in all honesty. With Ozzy delivering a sometimes hard to decipher lyric about having to leave his unhappy and stressful situation behind him, Iommi's accompanying guitar riffs are satisfyingly churning, but ultimately a little one-dimensional sounding. Oddly enough, there is a chorus in the song that offers a respite from the leaden riffery, and actually has some melodic appeal, which could have led to some commercial success, but it is unaccountably used only once during the song. By no means a poor track, it is nevertheless one of the less memorable moments on the album.

'Changes'

After 'Planet Caravan' and 'Solitude' on the previous two albums, it was becoming seemingly the done thing for Sabbath to include an acoustic or balladic song on their albums, and 'Changes' has, over the years, become one of the most divisive songs in the whole catalogue, with as many fans seemingly loving it as those who regard it otherwise. When the band were getting material together, during the cocaine-fuelled time in their large rented house, Tony Iommi found himself drawn to the grand piano that was located there, and during some long sleepless nights, he began teaching himself to play in a rudimentary fashion. As a result of those lone piano sessions, he came up with the music for 'Changes', to which Butler added despairing words inspired by Bill Ward's recent break-up (though, ironically, Ward does not appear on the track). Ozzy heard the song and immediately loved it, and indeed this coaxed one of his most heartfelt vocal performances out of him. The lush string accompaniment was added by Geezer Butler using a Mellotron, which, again, he had just about taught himself to use. The band had become friendly with Rick Wakeman at the time, from touring with Yes in support, and there was the opportunity to have him play the piano part, as indeed a string section could also have been sourced if needed. In the event, they wanted to supply all of the instrumentation themselves if at all possible, and, in fact, Wakeman himself admitted that he liked what Iommi had done.

Altogether, it really should not work as the piano accompaniment is basic at best, while the lyrics are not what could be described as particularly subtle or poetic. However, it was this very simplicity that enabled the song to pull at the heartstrings in its raw, honest way, and when Ozzy wails the heavily echoed chorus line 'I'm going through Changes', you really believe in him. The song even went on to become a big hit decades later for Ozzy, who performed a duet with his daughter, Kelly, with revised words. All in all, for a song that was written and performed by players unused to the instruments, and out of character for the band, it became an unexpected triumph.

'FX'
From triumph to disaster: safe to say, 'FX' was a stoned idea that should never have got beyond the joking stage. The idea for the track was conceived when Iommi's cross struck his fretboard while he was playing, and the effects-laden sound he was using gave it an otherworldly quality. So taken were the other band members with this that, in their chemically enhanced state, they took turns striking the strings to see what sounds they could get, and recorded it. Somehow, it was deemed album material. The best that can be said is that at less than two minutes in duration, it is mercifully brief.

'Supernaut'
In his autobiography, Ozzy Osbourne claimed that when he listens to this song even today, he can practically taste the cocaine. It is easy to believe as the sheer adrenaline throughout this track is utterly remarkable. The main riff that kicks the song off, delivered like a buzzsaw by Iommi, is a classic in itself, but the churning repeating figure that comes in four times before each verse is heavy on a previously unheard-of scale. However, whereas songs like 'Lord of this World' or 'Tomorrow's Dream' can almost collapse under the dirge-like heaviness and the dense rhythm section, 'Supernaut' seems to possess a spring-heeled quality throughout its entire length. It is hard to keep still when this song is playing, and a large part of the reason for that is the astonishing performance put in by Bill Ward. He drives the song, and the beat, along like a hyperactive piledriver, and even makes the funky drum breakdown in mid-song work. Iommi's

solo sounds like the work of an adrenalized man searching to put extra notes and fills in as if the already fast pace is boring him, and the impression of constant barely contained energy is reinforced again and again. Ozzy, meanwhile, is in magnificent voice here, soaring above the music with a range that he is rarely given credit for. This album, and the two that followed, would contain the finest vocals of his career. The lyric, meanwhile, spins an intriguing if baffling tale of a man who has lived a thousand years and wants to 'climb up every mountain on the moon' and touch the sun without needing to fly. Again, certainly this is probably a drug-related lyric, but the closing line 'I've seen the future and I've left it behind' leaves the listener to wonder whether there is more to it than that. A great lyric, leaving much to interpretation. The word 'Supernaut' is used to refer to a psychedelic drug trip wherein the user appears weightless, but whether there is any correlation to this is unclear. Interestingly, both Frank Zappa and John Bonham named this as their favourite Black Sabbath track, and Bonham once jammed with the band on a version of the song, though the tapes are unfortunately believed lost.

'Snowblind'

The official 'cocaine song', and the track that was going to be the title of the album had the record company not got cold feet over the implications and insisted on a change. The term 'Snowblind' literally refers to a temporary blindness caused by light reflecting off snow, but of course the usage here is in reference to the nickname of cocaine as 'snow'. The lyric is quite clever, though, and mixes some subtly couched drug references with images and metaphors of snowflakes, icicles, and blindness, and as with so much of Geezer Butler's best words, it remains fresh and does not pale no matter how many times you listen. Musically, the song is based around one of Iommi's simpler guitar riffs, but one that burrows into your brain and somehow stays there. The song is also lifted above the norm by small touches of brilliance—the use of guitar arpeggios in the lead-in and the brilliant 'My eyes are blind but I can see' slow passage for one, and the two masterful guitar solos for another (one coming in with perfect timing as Ozzy wails despairingly 'I feel the snowflakes freezing me!' and the other right after the final verse, and playing the track out). The band even use an orchestra in the end section of the track in another superb embellishment of the sound, subtle though it is. The orchestra had already been enlisted for the track 'Laguna Sunrise', and the brainwave occurred to use them here also. An interesting thing to note here is that, although the record company had blocked any direct drug references, and also censored the album title, if you listen closely to the end of the first verse, directly after the line 'Icicles within my brain', you can hear Ozzy whisper 'Cocaine' quietly but quite clearly. This was almost impossible to hear on original vinyl pressings of the album, but remastered CD editions have made it plain. Of course, when performing the song live, Ozzy would abandon all attempts to hide the fact by simply electing to bellow 'Cocaine!!' after every verse, which was perhaps not the same. The track was the only one from this album to remain in the set list as a long-term fixture, and it retains an imperceptible magic over and above many more immediately classic Sabbath tracks. A key song.

'Cornucopia'

Another peerless Butler lyric here, again with just the right measure of leaving things open to interpretation, while clearly offering a criticism of so-called modern material wealth, and the society that forces us to prize it. The 'cornucopia' was, of course, originally the Horn of Plenty in Greek myth, and as such is the perfect metaphor for the acquisition of more and more goods and status symbols to keep the populace happy and satisfied. Musically, there is an enormous amount going on here in just under four minutes, with the track moving from slow, grinding intro through frenetic verses, a slow, heavy chorus, and an entirely separate fast mid-section. While all of the song's disparate elements are excellent, and dovetail together extremely well, the real classic moment occurs just once, with Iommi's irresistible, charging bridging riff in between the first two verses, which is never repeated. The momentum produced at that point is quite astonishing. Once again, Bill Ward excels on drums, with much of the song being helped along by his driving hi-hat and cymbal work, while he even adds enormous gravitas and bombast at one point by the use of a gong. Another song that is relatively unexplored by most compilations and discussions of the band's finest moments, and yet it is a genuine high point among the many on this album.

'Laguna Sunrise'

Possibly emboldened by the acceptance of 'Orchid' on the previous album, Tony Iommi again tries his hand at an acoustic guitar instrumental, only this time longer, grander, and more fully realised. Conceived while watching the sun cope up at Laguna Beach during an all-night stay there with road manager Spock Wall, the central figure of the tune, which is what was brought back from that beachfront inspiration, is an undeniably beautiful melody, perfectly executed as an overdubbed guitar piece. Iommi and Wall also attempted to do the orchestral arrangement for the track, as it had been conceived with that in mind from early in the process, but when the orchestra came in to work on the song, they were unable or unwilling to work from the written arrangement they were given, and outside assistance had to be brought in to write out their parts to an acceptable standard. It was worth it, however, as the end result is a superb blending of the guitar and the orchestral strings. The same orchestra also contributed to 'Snowblind', as documented above.

'St Vitus Dance'

At less than two and a half minutes, one of the shortest of Sabbath's songs, this is nonetheless far from a throwaway piece. Indeed, driven along by an insidious, serpentine guitar figure and some infectiously upbeat rhythm work from Ward and Butler, it remains something of a mystery why this was never chosen as a single instead of 'Tomorrow's Dream' being the only track thus selected from the album. In the same way as 'Paranoid' managed to combine heaviness with a commercial feel, leading to its big singles chart placing, 'St Vitus Dance' combines a couple of big, sinister riffs with an overall spring in its step and an actual toe-tapping element unusual for the band. If it was conceived with commerciality in mind, it makes the decision not to launch it as a single all the more baffling. Lyrically, the song is very straightforward, with Ozzy advising his friend to go back to the woman he has split from, assuring him that she wants him and not, as he has believed, just his money. It is very similar to the narrative of the Beatles' 'She Loves You', leading to many speculating that the lyrics may be the work of Ozzy in this case, as he has always been known to be a huge Beatles fan. The title is something of a mystery, but there are different theories that have been put forward. St Vitus Dance itself is a neurological complaint, also known as Sydenham's Chorea, which causes uncontrollable jerking spasms, particularly of the hands and feet, making it appear as if sufferers are dancing (in the Middle Ages it was known as 'Dancing mania', and believed to be an affliction sent as a curse by St Vitus, hence the name). Some have theorised that the line 'You feel your nerves are shattering' provides the reference, though there is no universal agreement on whether that is indeed the correct transcription of the lyric, so that is vague at best. It has also been suggested that the danceable nature of the piece could lead to the, slightly tongue in cheek, title. It may also be that it is simply a random title, in a similar vein as 'N.I.B.'—as of this time, there is no consensus on the matter, and the band have not elaborated on it.

'Under the Sun'

Another track with an alternative 'extra' title, listed sometimes as 'Under the Sun'/'Every Day Comes and Goes' in reference to the midsection of the song containing that line, this closing track from the album is another massively heavy piece, and also quite a lengthy one at almost six minutes. Beginning with a trademark slow, lumbering Iommi riff, it soon morphs into another churning, insistent mid-tempo groove that Butler and Ward imbue with a marvellous feeling of a 'swing' to it. It is quite remarkably infectious, while also being anvil-heavy in execution—quite some balancing act to pull off, and one the band were never better at than on this album. The mid-section abruptly changes to an extremely up-tempo couple of verses, with Ozzy delivering the lines so fast as to be hard to decipher at times. When the big riff comes in again, however, it comes as a massive relief of tension, and is perfectly judged. As with 'Wheels of Confusion', there is again a coda to the piece, with a slower, descending chord progression and Iommi overlaying some great guitar work. The last thirty seconds of the track consist of the progression repeatedly slowed down more and more until a final run-through, which is so slow as to evoke glacial erosion, ends with a sudden climactic power-chord. Meanwhile, the lyrics rail against organised religion and people being told what to do by preachers, religious demagogues, and anyone seeking to control people's minds. An inspired way to close an album, which is without doubt among the finest of the band's career, and which some would argue remains their peak.

5

Sabbath Bloody Sabbath

Release date: 1 December 1973 (UK), 1 January 1974 (US)—the album was delayed owing to a vinyl shortage at the time.

Record Label: WWA (UK), Warner Brothers (US)

Personnel: Ozzy Osbourne, Tony Iommi, Geezer Butler, Bill Ward

The band originally started work on the album in Los Angeles, intending once more to record at The Record Plant. However, as well as the distractions that were threatening to derail the process, it turned out that changes to the studio—in particular, a huge synthesiser installed by Stevie Wonder—meant it was too small for them to use, and so they relocated to the UK. They rented Clearwell Castle in Gloucestershire and began rehearsals there. Allegedly haunted, the band members claim that they saw unexplained apparitions while they were there, and that the place had an alarmingly creepy presence and atmosphere about it. Black Sabbath simply did not just decamp to a studio to rehearse and record in a straightforward way at this point.

Ideas were proving hard to come by for Iommi, however, despite the move, and he admits now that he was suffering the worst case of 'writer's block' of his entire career. As time went on, with no material forthcoming, both Osbourne and Butler became concerned for the future of the band. When the breakthrough came, it was the main riff of the title song that opened the floodgates, and coincided with them opting to try playing in the particularly gloomy and unnerving location of the castle dungeons. Ozzy, in his autobiography, credits the Golden Earring album *Moontan* as being a catalyst in Iommi's renewed inspiration, as he claims that they were listening to the album when it triggered something in the guitarist's brain. Whatever the truth of that, once he recovered his riff-writing 'mojo', both he and the band were off and running.

Interestingly enough, none of this album stayed in the band's set lists for very long. By the time of their *Technical Ecstasy* tour of three years later, nothing from *Sabbath Bloody Sabbath* was included, making it the only unrepresented album in their catalogue at that point. With the material finally worked out, the recording took place in September 1973 at Morgan Studios in London, and when finally released at the end of that year, the album reached No. 4 in the UK and No. 11 in the US: their highest UK chart placing since *Paranoid*.

Rightly regarded as one of the band's finest ever album covers—and many would say the very best—the cover artwork was done by American artist Drew Struzan on behalf of the design company Pacific Eye and Ear. Still at a relatively early stage in his career, Struzan would go on to do the artwork for Alice Cooper's *Welcome to My Nightmare* among many others, while in the late 1970s and beyond, he became a sought-after designer of movie posters, including such film franchises as *Star Wars*, *Back To The Future*, and *Indiana Jones*. The brief for the front and back covers of *Sabbath Bloody Sabbath* was to depict a man dying a horrific death on the front and a more peaceful demise on the back, and he rose to this challenge in magnificent style. The front cover shows a man on a bed being tormented by real or imagined demons in human form, while the head of the bed is a skull that extends arms around the whole gruesome tableau. On the reverse, against a white background as opposed to the black of the front, the man is seen lying in bed surrounded by grieving family members, in a scene that suggests he has led a wealthy and happy life, while a strange figure of a man (with head out of shot) extends its arms as if to welcome him.

In the UK, there was also a gatefold cover that was not reproduced in the US for some odd reason, with a photo on the inner of the four band members from the waist up, superimposed translucently against what is intended to be an old period bedroom complete with four poster bed and bookcase full of old books. However, the effect is spoiled slightly by the presence of an electrical plug socket clearly visible on one wall. In the photo, Iommi (along with Ward and Butler) is covering his lower face with his arm, and some have suggested that this was because he had shaved off his trademark moustache at this point, and it was decided not to draw attention to the fact. Whether or not this is true, the band's appearance at this time at the California Jam festival does support the shaving part of the story. For whatever reason, Ozzy is the odd man out in the picture, with his face fully visible. Also included in the UK, but not in the US, was a paper inner sleeve with the lyrics and musician credits for each track. Ozzy was later on record as saying that he 'absolutely loved' the cover.

Songs

'Sabbath Bloody Sabbath'

The song that cured the writer's block, and what a way to get over it. The opening riff, the thing that rescued Iommi's muse, is simply massive. Opening with it played once only unaccompanied on the guitar before the band crash in, it is a huge statement of intent in both musical and lyrical terms. Butler has stated that the song was written about the good times and the bad times of being in Sabbath, and directed at the management, business people and everyone else who had tried to make things difficult for them—basically one big 'backs to the wall rant', as he has described it. The song uses light and shade in extreme form, as the pounding verses give way to the delicate chorus, with some extremely un-Sabbath-like light jazz-bluesy guitar underpinning the vocals. After the second chorus, there is a genuinely classic Sabbath moment as, with the music building back up to the riff again, Ozzy yells 'You bastards!' in what sounds like pent-up fury, as the angry-sounding guitar solo kicks in. Perfect timing—if that is not an adlib, it really deserves to be. After the guitar solo, the song segues into a slower, grungy riff accompanied by some astonishingly high-register Ozzy vocals. Some fans love this closing section (which was omitted from many live performances), but I find that it drags the track down somewhat, and ends, with another short guitar solo section following it, as something of an anti-climax.

'A National Acrobat'

This marks the point when Geezer Butler's lyrics truly reached another level of sophistication and subtlety. Full of impenetrable imagery and metaphor (and a baffling title), the song deals with the philosophical and theological implications of conception and reincarnation—quite some achievement for what most people regarded as just 'that heavy metal band from Birmingham'. Musically, the song is the band at their most 'progressive', going through a set of labyrinthine changes along its six-minute length. Heavy enough in tone, it is far from a brutal riff-fest, as the opening section of the song is driven along by a marvellously serpentine double-tracked guitar figure from Iommi, with Ozzy again putting in a superb vocal performance—his voice was never stronger than during this period. This riff was, according to Iommi's autobiography, unusually written by Geezer, with himself 'just adding bits to it'. After around the two-minute mark, things descend into an eerily atmospheric mid-section, with sparse guitars drenched in reverb accompanying some truly thought-provoking lyrical imagery. Just as this section threatens to outstay its welcome, the third 'part' of the track takes over with, firstly, an infectious, sprightly instrumental break similar to the coda of 'Wheels of Confusion', driven along by some exceptional drum-work from Ward and then closing things completely with a heavy closing section somewhat reminiscent of the closing part of the classic Black Sabbath itself. Not a track to stand out as an initial favourite on the album, its adventurous construction and wealth of different ideas gives it a longevity and fascination, which leaves it as a standout long after some of the other pieces on the album have begun to pale. A triumph of both composition and musicality, which the band were given scant credit for at the time.

'Fluff'

Another Iommi instrumental firmly in the 'Laguna Sunrise' mode, this gorgeously delicate piece features Iommi himself on acoustic and steel guitars, as well as piano and harpsichord, with only Geezer's bass accompanying him on this rather impressively virtuoso outing. The piece lifts itself up another notch when some beautifully played steel guitar paints details above the main theme in the way that a fine artist would render clouds—these parts are quite evocative of

Fleetwood Mac's classic 'Albatross' to these ears. It could perhaps be said that, at just over four minutes, the track slightly over-extends itself, but it is, for all that, a superb composition, and the equal to 'Laguna Sunrise'. The track was actually named as a nod to DJ Alan 'Fluff' Freeman, who not only championed the band, but also featured 'Laguna Sunrise' as the theme music to his BBC Radio show for a time. Another interesting fact is that, when Tony Iommi married for the second time, 'Fluff' was played as the couple walked down the aisle. Well, 'Into the Void' would not really do it, would it?

'Sabbra Cadabra'

It is quite hard to know exactly what to make of this song. On the face of it, there is nothing to it except a simple love story, but it almost seems too simplistic for the way Geezer was writing on this album. The song starts with a fast Iommi riff, with overlaid guitar line taking the song along with quite a jaunty feel; reminiscent of 'St Vitus Dance' from the previous album in some ways, Ozzy gleefully delivers cheerful lines about this 'lovely lady' who is 'always on my mind', and so on. However, at just two minutes into this six-minute track, the mood abruptly changes: as Ozzy delivers the line 'Good to know that she's all mine' at the end of the second chorus, the music suddenly drops to a slow, chugging grind, with Rick Wakeman adding piano and also his trademark synth flourishes. Ozzy's voice comes back in, heavily treated to give it a sinister quality, singing about how he is never going to leave her, 'any more, I said no more, no more...' etc., while the guitar and piano relentlessly drive the accompaniment on, becoming more and more insistent while the rhythm continues repetitively and incessantly. Eventually, Ozzy seems to leave the lyrics behind, just endlessly repeating 'no more, I said no more' etc., before finally ending with what sounds like maniacal chuckling low in the mix. The music by now has built to a sort of crescendo, still with that nagging rhythm, before it abruptly breaks down at the end. Many have speculated that there may be something more sinister at play here, in that the relationship perhaps changes as does the music, from happy and carefree to somewhat obsessed 'stalker', or controlling behaviour, to what, exactly? We do not know, as the band have never, to my knowledge, elaborated on this, but the speculation certainly gives the song a fascination and gravitas that it otherwise would not have. Then again, it has also been reported that engineer Tom Allom had to use heavy phasing effects on Ozzy's voice right at the end to conceal his profane language, so who really knows! Once more, the title is mystifying, as its play on 'abracadabra', and the magic associated with that phrase, may be simply a joke or may point to something within the song. Meanwhile, Wakeman's guest appearance on this track was so successful that the band would start using a regular guest keyboard player from the next album, albeit standing unseen in the wings at gigs.

'Killing Yourself to Live'

Along with the title track, the nearest thing on the album to a traditional Black Sabbath riff-based pounder. The lyrics were, according to Geezer, written while he was hospitalised for kidney problems caused by heavy drinking, and this theme certainly informs the song deeply. The overall message seems to be to warn against being trapped in a mundane position, and to avoid the obvious temptation to cope with this sort of life through excessive drugs or alcohol abuse. Musically, again, the song is a multi-part piece, changing as it goes along rather than going into a mid-section before returning to the main theme, which had been common on earlier albums. After a heavy riffing introduction, the verses come in accompanied by a slightly edgy, unsettling guitar line from Iommi, while the chorus is as near as the album gets to the 'wall of noise' heavy chording so prevalent on *Volume 4*. After the second chorus, and a double-tracked guitar solo, the song changes tack, with Ozzy growling the words 'Smoke it … Get high!' as a different riff enters the picture—this, if nothing else, seems to reinforce Geezer's assertion that substance abuse of whatever type was in his mind when writing the lyric. Finally, the song's climactic section comes into play at around the four-minute mark, with a blindingly fast riff and equally speedy Osbourne delivery of the final two verses leading us into another guitar solo, heavily multi-tracked this time, before the song grinds to an abrupt halt. A very strong track, without doubt, and the favourite of many who were unsure about some of the experimentation so prevalent throughout the album.

'Who Are You'

An unusual song in more ways than one: it is almost entirely synthesiser-based and it was actually composed by Ozzy, as

by both himself and Iommi in their respective
es. Ozzy remembers that he was 'fiddling around with a
ichine and an ARP 2600 synth', while Tony states that
ht synthesisers and Ozzy figured out to play one just
e up with the basis for 'Who Are You'. It sounds a little
is again playing some of the synths, but if so, then it
d, as the notes on the album's inner sleeve list Geezer
ing the synths (along with Mellotron by Geezer also).
nly a creepy atmosphere present in the song and the
n, and the mood fits the album perfectly, but overall, it
cperiment than a classic.

Today'

Another up-tempo song, with one of Iommi's upbeat, cheery sounding
guitar lines, the song deals with the temporal nature of fame or success,
with countless metaphors for things being old news almost as soon as
they are produced. It is a well-written lyric, dealing with the subject in
quite a literate way, but it does not have the depth of some of the other
weighty themes on the album. Similarly, the music has a little bit of a
light, almost throwaway quality about it. There are interesting things
going on—for example, Iommi's flute playing adding excellent colour
to the quiet, restrained choruses, but by the time the track fades out
after a lengthy coda, with Ozzy repeating the title seemingly endlessly,
accompanied by handclaps and an unexceptional Iommi solo, one is
left with a little bit of a feeling of filler about the track. Not bad, but
along with 'Who Are You', definitely putting a dent in the second half
of the album.

'Spiral Architect'

Now this is much more like it! After a couple of slightly sub-par
tracks, the album closes with a definite classic, both lyrically and
musically. The lyrics clearly refer to DNA, by way of the 'spiral', and,
indeed, Geezer did state in the liner notes to the *Reunion* album that
the song was 'about life's experiences being added to a person's DNA
to create a unique individual'. He has also claimed that the lyric was
initially inspired by a dream he had. Whatever the truth, it is a quite
stunning lyric, full of ambiguous metaphor and imagination-firing
imagery, and the fact that people are still debating its meaning speaks

volumes for its enduring fascination and power. Interpretations have ranged from the song being from the viewpoint of God or, conversely, Satan to theories that it is about film and television, taking its title from the old spirals of film. Musically, the mood is fit perfectly, as it mirrors the 'spiralling' effect uncannily, particularly at the end of each chorus; just as Ozzy sings 'You know that I should', the strings used so brilliantly on the track carry it upward to hit the guitar line that finishes the spiral. The track is far from a typical Sabbath song, with a bedrock of acoustic guitars along with the string section generating most of the power and propulsion of the music, in an almost orchestrally classical way. The strings (credited as 'The Phantom Fiddlers') were arranged by British composer, arranger, and producer Wil Malone, who has since gone on to work with, among others, Iron Maiden and also Opeth's 2016 album *Sorceress*, as well as a couple more Sabbath albums. One or two of the credits on the album's inner sleeve about this track are worthy of note: Geezer Butler is credited as 'bass/nose', which is one of the odder instrumental credits I can recall, and also Tony Iommi is credited with bagpipes, which is unconfirmed. Indeed, in his autobiography, Iommi claims he bought the bagpipes but failed to be able to play them, while it is hard to pick them out on the track. Nonetheless, a brilliant song to bring an audaciously experimental album to a close—one that is more complex than any Sabbath album to that point (or possibly ever), and yet one that just lacks the consistent brilliance of one or two others. One of which was lined up next.

6

Sabotage

Release date: 28 July 1975 (US), 22 August 1975 (UK)
Record Label: NEMS (UK), Warner Brothers (US)
Personnel: Ozzy Osbourne, Tony Iommi, Geezer Butler, Bill Ward

This album was recorded during the period January to March 1975 at Morgan Studios once again, following a lengthy period in 1974 when the band had been unable to work owing to enormous managerial and business troubles. While recording the *Sabbath Bloody Sabbath* album, they began to become aware of perceived unfair financial treatment at the hands of manager Patrick Meehan and, with relations between them and Meehan having become increasingly strained for some time, they sought to extricate themselves from their management contract with him. This led to seemingly endless to-ing and fro-ing of writs and lawsuits between the two parties, with the small matter of the music being caught in the crossfire. Indeed, even while they were recording *Sabotage*, Ozzy remembers writs actually being delivered to the mixing desk while they were attempting to work. This hassle led to the title of the album, as they felt that they were being sabotaged at every turn, and also to the vitriolic final track 'The Writ'. One upshot of all of this was yet another new record label, after one album on WWA Records, with this one appearing via NEMS in the UK. The album was this time co-produced by Tony Iommi and Mike Butcher, who had also worked as producer and engineer on *Sabbath Bloody Sabbath*. The album reached a healthy No. 7

in the UK album charts, but in the US, it peaked at a disappointing No. 28. For the tour following the album, a keyboard player was used for the first time, with another local Birmingham musician Gerald 'Jezz' Woodroffe stepping in, although playing out of sight in the wings.

From the sublime (*Sabbath Bloody Sabbath*) to the ridiculous, the *Sabotage* album cover is one that has been widely vilified and ridiculed ever since its appearance—sometimes even by the band members themselves. The original concept, proposed by Bill Ward's drum technician Graham Wright (a graphic artist himself) of the band being reflected in inverted form in a mirror has some merit. The band stand in front of the mirror, and their front, rather than back, is reflected, and *vice versa* on the rear, which is a thought-provoking image. The execution, however, was a disaster. The idea was for the band to be pictured in front of the mirror wearing all black costumes to be provided. They arrived for what, reportedly, was supposed to be a test shoot, only to be told that it was the actual session, and that the costumes had not been delivered and the band would have to wear whatever they had with them at the time. Ozzy is wearing a full-length kimono, and Tony (the only one seated) and Geezer are more conventionally attired, though the latter is oddly sporting a rolled-up umbrella. Bill Ward comes off the worst as he was wearing a pair of his wife's red tights at the time. In order to protect his modesty to some extent (and to make the shot usable), Ozzy reportedly lent him a pair of underpants, which can be clearly seen in all of their red and white checked glory on the back cover. The leather jacket he paired this ensemble with did not do him any favours either. Add to this catalogue of farce the fact that there were inconsistencies in the photo shoot; on the back cover, Geezer's 'rear reflection' shows his left arm straight, whereas it was in his jacket pocket on the front. Ozzy is similar, as the angle of his head is noticeably different on the back to the pose on the front. It was all rushed, to say the very least, and there were some promises that the worst excesses of the photos would be airbrushed out later. Of course, they were not, and the band were aghast when they saw the finished item. Coupled with this was the fact that the cover featured no gatefold or inner sleeve, completing this most basic and unfortunate package. A little bit of smoke wisping in the bottom corner, presumably in a belated and desperate attempt to create some 'atmosphere', could be generously described as being 'too little, too late'. The music was going to have to be great to compensate for this. Fortunately, it was.

Songs

'Hole in the Sky'

An absolutely massive way to open the album. Beginning with a little bit of background studio noise and a voice (allegedly either Bill Ward or a studio tech) shouting what sounds like 'Attack!!', the whole band swing in together with a huge, piledriving gut-punch of a riff. Sabbath songs do have a tendency to start with the guitar riff unaccompanied before the band join, but here the effect of them all hitting the ground running, so tight that it would be hard to slip a cigarette paper between them, is stunning. The main riff is remarkable in the way that it lopes along at a mid-to-fast paced tempo, with a real swing provided by Ward's superb drum work, and yet is simultaneously skull-crushing in effect. There are numerous great moments during this track, but one of them comes courtesy of another moment of Ozzy magic at the end of the second chorus, where he finishes 'Through which I'll fly … YEAH!' just as Iommi launches into the double-tracked guitar solo. Nobody, but nobody, could make the word 'Yeah', or variants thereof, sound as great as Ozzy at this time. Lyrically obtuse (as is much of this album), the meaning of the track has been debated for years, with differing interpretations including living in prison, watching TV, apocalyptic destruction (ah yes, that old friend again), or a man at the end of his life realising that all has been futile and he now waits for the end to see what comes after. This last interpretation gains some traction from the sudden and abrupt ending, mid-riff, as if he has suddenly died. Whatever the interpretation, this is powerful stuff.

'Don't Start (Too Late)'

Another Iommi acoustic guitar showcase, this is a much shorter example of that form, coming in at under a minute, but it has some of his fastest and cleanest picking yet. There is a clever, repeated, spiralling little part, which at the end of the track brings us down and down until it leads exactly into the steam-hammer riff introducing the timeless third track. The title of this piece, incidentally, comes from the despairing cry supposedly uttered by studio engineer Robin Black whenever the band began playing too soon, which was apparently a regular occurrence.

'Symptom of the Universe'

The song chosen to open the shows on the 1977 and 1978 tours, 'Symptom of the Universe' is simply magnificent in its unstoppable skull-bashing fury. Opening with the iconic riff ground out with an incredibly ferocious and meaty guitar tone, when the band come in, especially Ward's drums, it takes the listener by the lapels and dares you not to love it. The riff is slightly reminiscent of Queen's track 'Stone Cold Crazy' from the year before, but slowed down in tempo to the sweet spot where the cartoon thrashiness of the Queen song becomes genuine, brutal, ball-crushing metal. The bridging riff contains some astonishing drum fills from a manic-sounding Ward, and Ozzy's trademark cries of 'Yeahhhhh!' after each verse are as effective as they always seem to be. At the end of the third verse, the tempo shifts up for a tremendous Iommi solo, which clips along at a galloping pace before then abruptly slowing out of seemingly nowhere for an incongruous coda with acoustic guitars and a jazzy, improvised feel. This section, which takes care of the final two minutes of the six here, was never played live by the original foursome, and it does feel a little odd in contrast with the rest of the song, but it is nice enough, with a loose jam feel to it (allegedly it was indeed born from a studio jam). Lyrically, there is some consensus, albeit with disagreement around the fine detail of the words. It is accepted that it is, on the surface, a love song, but many interpret it as being specifically about birth, death, and reincarnation, with the 'symptom of the universe' itself being either love or the act of conception. A true classic, however you slice it.

'Megalomania'

Another masterpiece here, and one that is in many ways the centrepiece of the album; certainly the longest track, at nearly ten minutes. The title, of course, refers to the mental state characterised by ultimate delusions of grandeur or of one's own self-importance in the world, and Butler's lyrics take this as the starting point, but as so often, it leaves us unsure about some of the debatable inferences within the words. The song begins very eerily and menacingly, with an echoed voice emerging gradually from the depths repeating 'I hide I hide I hide I hide' before resolving into 'I hide myself inside the shadows of shame' (a trick used even more effectively before the second verse with 'Obsessed obsessed obsessed obsessed obsessed with fantasy…'). With a slow, heavy chorus interspersed with these verses, the song appears as if it is going to be following the simple 'quiet-loud-quiet' template until, after just over three minutes, Iommi kicks in with an insistent, propulsive guitar riff driving things along brilliantly. By the time the song ends, some six minutes later, with some unintelligible vocalising from Ozzy and a solo from Iommi, together with what sound like (uncredited) strings, the protagonist so mired within insanity at the start of the song is beginning to extol his 'escape' from the unknown subject, which has been variously been interpreted as drugs (causing the mental state), God/religion, Satan, or just his mental demons themselves. Live evidence of performances of this track indicate it as having been a phenomenal stage song, and it is a great shame that the song was retired from live performance after the immediate *Sabotage* tour.

'Thrill of it All'

A song that is basically spliced together from what seem like two different pieces, 'Thrill of it All' opens side two of the vinyl with a slow, plodding riff, briefly broken by an up-tempo teaser of what the second half of the track will become, before the juddering opening riff returns as Ozzy despairingly intones a couple of verses dealing with the problems of humanity. At just over two and a half minutes in, however, the track shifts gear, speeds up, and a driving, infectious synthesiser hook (played by Iommi) carries us along irresistibly. To match the music's change of mood, the lyrics appear to follow suit as Ozzy, in far more joyous voice, talks of forgetting 'your problems that don't even exist' and assuring us that 'you matter to me'. It may be that this is a Christian influence again coming in, in response to the question posed to Jesus in the opening section 'When you see this world we live in, do you still believe in man?'—although on the other hand it could just as easily be a call to humanity to embrace their own innate positivity and help themselves. Whatever the thinking behind it, this is, musically and lyrically, one of Sabbath's most uplifting tracks, and by the time the climactic guitar solo comes in, skittering joyfully across the soaring musical backdrop, the listener is carried along with it. There was a major problem while recording the song, however, as, after working extremely hard to finally nail the piece, the band were informed that the tapes were left unusable owing to a recording error and they had to redo the whole thing from scratch. This is the reason behind the credit on the album to 'Tape op and Saboteur—David Harris'. Possibly because of this experience, but more likely because of the dominant synthesiser work, the song was never played on stage. Even with Jezz Woodroffe in the wings adding keyboard colour to the performance, one might imagine that with such a dominant instrumental role on this song, it might draw too much attention to the 'unofficial' keyboardist.

'Supertzar'

Another Iommi track without lyrics here, but a very different beast from his acoustic guitar pieces 'Laguna Sunrise' or 'Fluff'. The song is driven along by an Eastern-European guitar riff evoking a dramatic, unstoppable marching feel, and is further lifted by the presence of the English Chamber Choir providing a massive, wordless vocal backdrop. This is quite unlike any other track in Sabbath's catalogue (or pretty much anybody's, come to that). Ozzy later commented on how impressive the track sounded, but at the time it was recorded, an amusing tale is recounted that he arrived at the studio while the track was being recorded, saw the choir, and also a harpist who had been enlisted, assumed he had come to the wrong studio and walked out again. In actual fact, the choir is once again arranged by Wil Malone, who had worked on the previous album. 'Supertzar' immortalised its place in the live environment by becoming Sabbath's intro music at shows right up to Ozzy's departure following the *Never Say Die* tour, and in the eyes of many fans, including this writer, it was one of the most evocative introductory pieces ever used—when this played and the house lights went down, the effect was electrifying. This is illustrated on the film of the Hammersmith show in 1978, titled *Never Say Die* and covered later in this book.

'Am I Going Insane (Radio)'

Easily the most light-hearted moment on the album, this is a somewhat atypical song for Black Sabbath in that it is essentially a rock song, but of a much more upbeat and pop-oriented variety than most—in the vein of 'St Vitus Dance' from *Volume 4*, in some ways. It opens with an uncharacteristic swirl of the guitars from Iommi, with a vaguely Spanish feel, continuing into the first verse. When the (admittedly very catchy) chorus enters the fray, it is introduced brilliantly by Ward, with a perfect drum fill seeming to catapult the listener in. Ward is also the architect of the second touch of genius in the chorus, as it is played out by an odd, echoing percussive effect. These things ensure that the song does not get as repetitive as it otherwise might. As the song fades out, maniacal laughter comes up higher and higher in the mix, only to devolve into some sinister wailing bridging into the following track—this was actually achieved by slowing down a recording of one of Ozzy's young children at the time crying. The greatest misconception about the track is that the 'Radio' subtitle refers to the song's commerciality or that it was a radio edit; in fact, it comes from the Cockney rhyming slang 'Radio rental', meaning 'mental'. Nonetheless, as if following that very subtitle, the track was released as a single, backed by 'Hole in the Sky'. Perhaps surprisingly, it failed to chart.

'The Writ'

As the tortured cries from the end of the previous track subside, their place is taken by a gently bubbling bassline; yet this calm does not last long as Ozzy's voice crashes in suddenly along with the full force of the band. Unusually, the lyrics to this song were written entirely by Ozzy himself, as a direct response to those parties who were giving them such grief and hassle with the various legal matters while recording was taking place. As the band sling out a violent and juddering riff, the words are practically spat out in a tirade of bitterness. There is very little to read into this song: it is a cry of frustration and fury, the intensity of which initially takes the listener's breath away. Midway through the track, however, things change once again and the mood shifts from vitriol to optimism. The music changes to a more upbeat tone, with Ozzy asserting that 'everything is gonna work out fine'. This is interspersed with two slightly oddly placed quietly sung and played verses, a little reminiscent of Alice Cooper's 'Only Women Bleed', before a final driving coda arrives quite briefly to fade out. It is certainly a very powerful piece, and a very honest one, but the construction of the song seems a little unbalanced, and the momentum is somewhat dissipated by the time the song winds to its close after eight minutes, providing a slightly anticlimactic ending to a magnificent album.

Hidden Track

'Blow on a Jug'

In one of the seemingly strangest moves on the part of a Sabbath album, after 'The Writ' comes to its conclusion, a brief snippet of a song entitled 'Blow on a Jug' emerges, with Bill Ward singing over a country blues 'jugband' accompaniment at very low volume. It is bizarre indeed, though reportedly there is a story behind it. Supposedly, at a 1970 festival, Sabbath were upstaged somewhat unexpectedly by Mungo Jerry, who featured a jug-player, much to Ozzy's chagrin. He was reportedly heard to fume 'We had no chance after that. Blowing on a fucking jug!!', and five years later, it was finally addressed.

7

Technical Ecstasy

Release date: 25 September 1976 (US), 8 October 1976 (UK)
Record Label: Vertigo (UK), Warner Brothers (US)
Personnel: Ozzy Osbourne, Tony Iommi, Geezer Butler, Bill Ward
                (plus Jezz Woodroffe)

Freed at last from the legal shackles that had tied their hands so badly
in terms of both live and studio work before and during the *Sabotage*
sessions, the band elected to record in America again, decamping to
Miami and booking into Criteria Studios. Featuring some changes in
approach once again, the album was credited as being produced by
the band, but in reality, this was reportedly Iommi to all intents and
purposes. Indeed, he has spoken about his frustration as the rest of
the band spent much of their time on the beach while he laboured
over the record. Cracks were starting to show in the band's solidarity,
with Ozzy in particular beginning to show some signs of losing the
plot slightly owing to drink and drugs—indeed, he checked himself
into Stafford County Asylum (also known by the less stark name of St
George's) on his return to England, though he did not last very long
in there. Part of the problem with the band at the time was that Ozzy
was starting to have ideas about a solo career, and had even taken to
appearing in public with a T-shirt bearing the name 'Blizzard of Ozz'.
It was destabilising for the band, and he in fact left for a time after
the tour to promote the album had been concluded. He was replaced
briefly by ex-Savoy Brown vocalist Dave Walker, but the band did

not record with him. The album still reached a fairly healthy No. 13 on the UK album chart, but in the US, it limped to No. 52 before dropping again.

If the *Sabotage* artwork was contentious, this was possibly even more so. In line with the album title, chosen in order to distance themselves a little from the old 'doomy, black magic' image, they enlisted legendary designers Hipgnosis to design the cover, with the result being accurately described by an unimpressed Osbourne as 'two robots screwing on an escalator'. Hipgnosis' Storm Thorgerson has defended the cover art, saying that it illustrated the concept of the title, and embodied the ecstasy in the form of a brief encounter by two robots passing each other on an escalator. Some fans were less impressed, however, with the change from black to a much brighter white and yellow-dominated colour scheme criticised as moving too far from their past. In reality, while not perfectly executed, it was an interesting idea and was continued in the programme for the tour promoting the album—inside the programme are drawings of the four members as robots, having work done on circuits in their heads. Had this been incorporated in the album package, it might have been a more effective and appealing design, but sadly the lack of a gatefold resulted in only a paper insert with red-on-blue lyrics against a background of robot blueprints. As an overall package, it can best be described as a brave failure—but it is hard to avoid the conclusion that the radical design image change may have hindered sales.

Songs

'Back Street Kids'
A high-energy start to the album, as the band crash in all together with a rampaging, galloping rhythm. After the initial riff, and a quick taster of what would be the backing to the chorus, Ozzy comes in with a lyric extremely true to the early days of the band, about growing up in the back streets of Birmingham with just the music to embrace as their own. Indeed, the feeling is that the opening lines 'I'm just another backstreet kid/Rock 'n Roll music is the only thing I really dig' is as close to a definitive life statement as Ozzy could ever deliver. The keyboards of Jezz Woodroffe make themselves felt right from the

word go here as, while the band had used synths previously, this was the first occasion where the keyboards were truly integrated into the music, rather than laid over the top. The slightly less dark and gloomy feel that pervades the album is evident immediately in this opening track, but the fact remains that it is an excellent opener, and when it abruptly comes to a sudden halt right at the end of the chorus line 'Nobody I know could ever take my rock and roll away from me', it leaves an almost breathless feel. On a lighter aside, it has been pointed out that, with the aforementioned chorus statement, Ozzy may find himself in trouble if anyone he does not know attempts to take his rock and roll away from him.

'You Won't Change Me'
The first really 'epic'-sounding piece on the album, this mid-paced and majestic song marks a real high point for the album. Again, the lyric does not have the impenetrable fascination of the last two or three albums, but here it is still extremely thought-provoking and well-written. The central character appears to be a man so afraid of change that he defiantly declares that nothing can change him, while musing on whether it might be a good thing if he were able to open up and accept other people into his desperately inward-looking and insular life. The second verse sees him extending this thought process, as he addresses the woman who wants to be close to him, musing about how he wonders 'what it's like to be loved', yet being unable to force himself to let that love into himself. A dismissive chorus sees him brushing aside these thoughts, as the line 'Nobody will change the way I feel' ushers in the first of two strident and expressive guitar solos in the song. However, a third and final verse sees him realising his predicament and imploring God to help him, while accepting that 'it may be that it's over for me', before that same chorus again seems to see him as a lost cause, as the climactic solo and instrumental section take over. It is a brilliantly delivered song, lyrically, and Ozzy, despite his voice showing signs of deterioration for the first time, does a magnificent job in putting it across. Once again, Woodroffe's keyboards are pivotal, particularly in a passage leading into the verses that sees him using the strident and arresting tones of what sounds like a church organ. A great song, and a sorely underappreciated one. As with the opener, and the album in general, the only thing really

to complain about is the production, which provides too much gloss and treble, while the bottom end—Sabbath's signature in the past—is disappointingly lacking.

'It's Alright'

A real oddity in the Sabbath catalogue, this song is not only sung by Bill Ward, but it was also mainly written by him, apart from some input from Iommi with the guitar parts. It is a peculiar song from a Sabbath point of view, with an entirely 'pop' approach, yet quite classily done—somewhat reminiscent of mid-period Beatles in some ways. The first verse comes in quietly before verse two is heralded by a massive drum fill right around the kit—oddly out of place yet enjoyable, and perhaps forgivable from a drummer on the first song he had written, it is a little like the famous Phil Collins drum break from 'In the Air Tonight', which would appear some years later: 'I've got a drum kit and I'm gonna use it', if you like. The song continues with a lyric that, though slightly confusing in one or two places ('It's always been this way and it can never be' for example), appears to be giving advice that once one embraces love, or even perhaps faith, and accepts that some things cannot be changed, then everything will, indeed, be 'alright'. It is quite uplifting and strangely comforting in a way. After a slightly odd multi-tracked guitar section in the middle of the song, which does smack of padding, Iommi contributes an unusual yet effective acoustic guitar solo towards the end. It has always been a divisive song, with some loving it and as many hating it among the fan base, but whatever the merits of the song in a compositional sense, it cannot be denied that Ward does an excellent job vocally. There are some high 'Woo-hoo' notes, which would perhaps have been better omitted, but in the main body of the song, when he is within his range, he does it well. Final verdict on the song? It is alright.

'Gypsy'

Another hugely dramatic song as a contrast to the previous track, 'Gypsy' tells the story, with just enough left implicit to make it intriguing, of a man encountering a mysterious gypsy who, having read his mind and not liking what she sees there, seems to slowly take him over, body, mind, and soul. The opening to the song, and the first verse, are quite upbeat and fast-paced, as if to illustrate the carefree frame of mind in which that the central figure begins the song, but this only lasts for the one verse before his encounter with the gypsy takes the music to an altogether darker and more sinister place as he realises she is 'the devil in drag' and 'the queen of all hell', yet cannot tear himself from her sinister influence. When the chorus 'So you want to be a gypsy' comes in, it is accompanied by some stunning Iommi guitar embellishments, scattering guitar licks like St Elmo's fire over the music and lifting it to another level of malice and intrigue, and when Ozzy finishes the final verse with a despairing 'As the sun shines on another day/You're gonna take my mind as well—it's over!', the effect is extraordinary. A climactic solo from Iommi takes the song to its conclusion, with staccato piano stabs all adding to the drama. One of the most overlooked and underappreciated of all Sabbath songs, it is a minor masterpiece and was showcased in the live set on the ensuing tour to marvellous effect, but sadly dropped from the repertoire thereafter.

'All Moving Parts (Stand Still)'

Another slight departure for the band here, as a grandiose opening gives way to a powerful, loping riff with a more loose, funky feel to it than anything the band had previously attempted. It works, however, as the song moves along as unstoppably as any of their heaviest tracks owing to the sheer power and effortless groove that they inject into the song. Lyrically, it is about a corrupt politician with odd sexual proclivities—according to Butler years later, he originally envisioned a transvestite President of the United States. Whatever the subject matter, the lyrics fit the music so well rhythmically that they complement it perfectly. A speedy, hard-rocking mid-section breaks things up, with a brief solo before the groove snaps back in to take the song to the end. One special mention should be given for the delicious relish Ozzy brings to the opening line of that middle eight: 'I like choking toys'—even if that is written by Butler, it will forever be Ozzy's line, like many lyrical phrases throughout his Sabbath career that he has made his own. A closing, frenzied guitar solo brings the song to a close, opening the old second side of vinyl with another excellent track. Like 'Gypsy', this was also played on the accompanying tour, but dropped thereafter.

'Rock and Roll Doctor'

Now, there is simple and there is simple. This good-time rock and roll boogie song, all barrelhouse piano and foot-stomping rhythm, may have some kind of throwaway charm, but it is easily the weakest song on the album. It has been suggested that the doctor in question was in fact a dealer, but it really does not add all that much interest either way. The strange thing about this track is that it not only made its way into the band's live set, but also stayed there for the following tour as well—the only track from this album to remain by then apart from the evergreen 'Dirty Women'. One can only assume they thought it was a good live sort of song. They may have been wrong, but that would be the assumption. Notably, the first short period of the track bears no resemblance whatsoever to the rest of the song, being as it is a dramatic introductory passage with a huge guitar solo that brings to mind Leslie West and his band Mountain. After twenty or so seconds, it simply devolves into a clichéd rocking lick and never reappears. An odd track all round, with the intro making it even odder.

'She's Gone'

This one is much better. Certainly not typical Sabbath by any stretch of the imagination, but this big, orchestrated, tragic love song is one of the band's most heartfelt ballads, and is a much more sophisticated cousin to the evergreen 'Changes'. Ozzy is in brilliant form here, and the way he delivers such lines as 'The silent emptiness of one-sided love' is positively heart-breaking. Interestingly, while 'Supertzar' was used as the band's intro music on the following couple of tours, this track was the song played over the PA as the audience filed out of the building at those shows, which was a perfect touch. One to play for someone who will not believe that Sabbath can do subtlety, emotion, and high-quality musicianship all together. They will believe it after this.

'Dirty Women'

Of all the songs on the album, this climactic ode to the hookers the band observed in Miami during the sessions for the album has remained the best-loved and best known, being included in the set at Ozzy shows right up until the present day. It is actually quite a multi-faceted song, beginning with alternating tempos as the opening verses set the scene, with the protagonist walking the damp, neon-lit streets in search of a woman who, if he finds one, will, he hopes, make everything all right. He finds a pimp with 'takeaway women for sale', and concludes that is the answer to his problems, as 'takeaway women don't fail'. The song then shifts up a gear with a short instrumental section and a brief 'jazzy-proggy' kind of feel before we are introduced to the central meat of the song—a driving beast of a riff that bears a slight nod to 'N.I.B.', and takes us into the heaviest part of the track, with Ozzy lasciviously exulting about how dirty women 'don't mess around'. We are not done with the changes, however, as this morphs into a slower, more reflective section, with Ozzy again musing that everything would be okay if he could only 'score' tonight, which leaves one with the distinct implicit impression that this does not, in fact, make everything okay at all, and takes us into a lengthy solo to play the track out; at over two minutes, this is Iommi's finest moment on the album, as the music builds and speeds up and drives the solo to its ever more frenetic conclusion. A classic track to close what is certainly not a perfect album, but is a strong one and much better than its sometimes poor reputation would suggest. A worthy addition to the band's catalogue, without doubt.

8

Never Say Die!

Release date: 28 September 1978
Record Label Vertigo (UK), Warner Brothers (US)
Personnel: Ozzy Osbourne, Tony Iommi, Geezer Butler, Bill Ward
              (plus Don Airey)

To say this album had a difficult gestation period would be putting things extremely mildly. Ozzy had left the band after the *Technical Ecstasy* tour and, not knowing if or when he would be back, the band recruited Dave Walker, who had sung with Savoy Brown and Fleetwood Mac among others, to replace him. While Walker was with the band, they did not record anything, though they did appear on a UK television show called *Look Hear* on 6 January 1978, performing 'War Pigs' and an early version of 'Junior's Eyes' with different lyrics. They did write a few songs with Walker, but when Ozzy eventually returned towards the end of January, he refused to sing any of them. As the band were due to go into the studio in three days' time to start recording, that left them with something of an issue to put it mildly. They went to record the album at Sound Interchange studios in Toronto, but immediately found another problem when the studio sound turned out to be all wrong for what they required. They improved matters by taking up the studio carpets, but it still was not perfect. They were rehearsing and writing new material during the day, in a freezing cold converted cinema, and then recording at night. With drink and drug issues still widespread within the band, and their focus somewhat less than total, sessions dragged on until May amid an increasingly tense atmosphere. The album reached No. 12 on the UK chart, keeping up a reasonably consistent performance, but in the US, it only managed a very disappointing No. 69.

Enter the Hipgnosis team again, who produced a rather strange cover image of Second World War pilots wearing full body suits and oddly sinister-looking masks (which, it has been claimed, were actually oxygen masks used by mountaineers). There are also faint, ghostly images in the clouds on the front and back. It has been asserted that these include the Grim Reaper and Winston Churchill, but they are quite indistinct. It has even been interpreted that the ghostly images are the pilots who have died, and the suits are continuing without them. There was no gatefold, but there was an inner sleeve with the original vinyl, containing some blueprints of Second World War aeroplanes and the album credits, but no lyrics this time. Interestingly, Hipgnosis originally offered the band the photo of the surgeons in masks—which went on to be used for Rainbow's album *Difficult to Cure*—but they turned it down, which is in retrospect probably not a bad decision as that picture would arguably have been a worse fit for a Sabbath cover than the one eventually used on this album.

Songs

'Never Say Die'
The title track to the album (though for some reason without the exclamation mark that the album title possesses, which we probably do not need to explore) opens up proceedings in fine style. The band crash in all together in a simple, but wonderfully infectious, four-chord sequence. Ozzy sounds positively joyful as he puts everything into the vocal, and when released as a single (with 'She's Gone' on the B-side), it became Sabbath's first UK hit single since 'Paranoid', reaching No. 21. At last! They even performed it on the BBC's *Top of the Pops* television show. The lyric is a relatively straightforward appeal to not give up whatever the odds, but does contain some interesting imagery ('Truth is on the doorstep/Welcoming the lies') to keep it a cut above the common denominator, as are most Black Sabbath lyrics, though they often do not get the credit they deserve for this quality. Interestingly, and perhaps tellingly, this was the only song to make its way into the live set list for the accompanying tour. An excellent way to open the album.

'Johnny Blade'

A surprisingly direct lyric to this one, telling the story of Johnny, a knife-wielding troublemaker who, it is implied, will end up meeting an unpleasant end himself. As relatively simple as the words may be, however, musically, the song is fairly sophisticated, going through some changes over its six-and-a-half-minute duration. The opening is a somewhat strange keyboard introduction, played by future Rainbow and Deep Purple man Don Airey, who provided keyboards throughout the record. Pretty soon it morphs into the first section proper, with Ozzy setting the scene over an up-tempo backing, with Iommi's serpentine, distorted guitar line driving things along. After a couple of minutes, things slow to a more archetypal Sabbath plod, as the tempo slows and Ozzy gets a little more sinister expression into it as he reveals the background to Johnny's lifestyle. A couple of keyboard flourishes take us into the final verses with a warning of Johnny's likely fate before a lengthy instrumental section gives us an excellent extended Iommi solo with some great work by Bill Ward. A good, and interesting, song.

'Junior's Eyes'

A song that was initially written with Dave Walker, with entirely different words, this finished version has a superb lyric by Butler written for Ozzy's father, who had just passed away. The song opens with a sparse, jazzy introduction driven by the bass and drums before the guitar enters, splashing colour all over the piece with chords drenched in echo and reverb. From this miasma of sound, Ozzy enters with the first verse, the lyric clearly very personal for him, and when the chorus arrives, it is a big, power-chord driven one, before we drop down to the sparsely accompanied verses again, which have an almost Led Zeppelin-like feel to them as Iommi's echoey chords are reminiscent of those used by Jimmy Page on several occasions. The chorus is mighty each time it arrives, and in fact more and more so as Iommi drapes each succeeding chorus repetition with ever more fiery guitar lines. An instrumental section in the middle is lit up by one of the most melodic and emotional solos Iommi has committed to tape for quite some time, and as Ozzy ends each chorus with the line 'I'll try my hardest not to cry when it is time to say goodbye', the effect is simultaneously musically powerful and emotionally moving. A top-quality track, often unappreciated, and one that can make a good argument for being the best song on the album. Interestingly, there was an English band named Junior's Eyes in the late '60s, who included Tim Renwick, later to work with The Sutherland Brothers and Quiver and Pink Floyd among others. They released an album, *Battersea Power Station*, in 1969, around the time Earth were becoming Black Sabbath, but whether there is any connection with the title has never been made clear.

'Hard Road'

Another track released as a single, the second from the album, it sneaked into the UK Top 40, perhaps aided by a limited purple vinyl release, but failed to make much impression. In a way, it was a good choice as a single as the chord progression powering the track is infectious and upbeat, and the chorus is quite memorable. The song has a positive message to fit the music as well, indicating that, while life (and probably their time in the band as well) can be a hard road, it does not need to be. It was too long, however, and does run out of steam somewhat by the end of its almost six-minute length. As a side note, this track marks the one and only time Tony Iommi actually sings on a Black Sabbath track, contributing backing vocals towards the end of the song. A video for the track was made during the tour following the album's release, appearing as if the band are performing it, though it was not actually in fact played live. Again, it is an enjoyable track, however, and brings to a close a very strong first side of the original vinyl album. Side two would bring some much more varied, and at times controversial, material.

'Shock Wave'

Another hard-rocking track, but overall a fairly undistinguished one. Iommi produces some nice guitar work (though his tone is uncharacteristically metallic and bright sounding), and Ward is exceptional, but the lack of any sort of decent melody is glaringly obvious as Ozzy meanders through the song, unable to get his teeth into any of the verses (with the one exception of the 'Look behind you!' line, which works brilliantly). The lyrics are slightly odd, in that at times they appear to be about cryogenics, and the character in the song opting to freeze his body when he realises he is about to die, but then it veers off course somewhat and seems to be describing more of a nightmare situation. Not a bad listen, but unsatisfying—and the 'Hoo-hoo' backing vocals towards the end should frankly never have been allowed to come within a mile of a Black Sabbath song.

'Air Dance'

The first real oddity on the album, this song is the jazziest thing the band had done to date, though it does go through some changes over its duration. The intro to the song is an excellent piece of instrumental bravado, sweeping the song in on a wave of expectation, but it is then never returned to, as the song proper comes in on a much lower-key note. Over just two verses and two choruses, the lyrics paint a moving picture of an ageing dancer looking back over her life and remembering the dancing she can now only do in her imagination. Ozzy does a reasonable job outside of his comfort zone, and the verses work very well, although the chorus strays dangerously close to cheesy dinner-jazz. Singing done, the song takes us into a pure jazz instrumental mid-section before Iommi's guitar solo in the climax of the piece sees him planting both feet straight into jazz fusion territory. He does it with some aplomb, but the song is a slightly uncomfortable mix of parts that do not entirely gel together. Certainly interesting to listen to, however, and a brave experiment for sure. For Sabbath, though, many felt this was like a jazz band suddenly plugging in distortion pedals and covering Grand Funk Railroad songs: even if you can do it, people do not generally want you to.

'Over to You'

Here we see one of the strongest lyrics on the album, with a message, and in some cases a structure, very reminiscent of John Lennon's classic 'Working Class Hero'. It begins with the protagonist bemoaning the fact that he was so trusting of the lying and deceiving school system that he 'handed my childhood over to you'. He then goes on to extend this metaphor to his being an adult, lied to and controlled by the same faceless system, and this time handing his future over to them. He briefly shows some resistance as he imagines the politicians or other controlling figures themselves falling on hard times, and that he can then hand their empty promises over to them. By the end, however, he has apparently lost hope as he hands his children 'over to you', and finishes on the despairing line 'All over. Over to you'. It is bleak stuff for sure, and pretty well constructed, but once again the music just cannot do the lyric the justice it deserves to really make it come alive. The main verses are delivered against an insistent rolling progression, which is nice but really only adequate, but then it goes into other sections that veer into light Genesis territory, with a tinkling piano from Airey dribbling all over Ozzy's vocal like some ghastly Liberace arrangement. It is a shame as this really cries out for more than the uninspiring treatment it receives. Talking of uninspiring, the next track leaves a lot to be desired.

'Breakout'

Ah, yes: the 'jazz instrumental', the horn section. This was the track that had Ozzy finally saying enough was enough and that they had crossed the line. The story goes that he saw all of these horn players trooping into the studio and he simply walked out, memorably commenting later that if that was the direction they were going in, they might as well have been called 'Slack Haddock, not Black Sabbath'. The thing is, he is really not wrong. It is not so much that this is horn-led jazz, it is not even good horn-led jazz. A dismal and tedious rising and falling crescendo figure forms the backdrop to a saxophone solo, which gives saxophone solos a bad name—which is saying something! This really should have stayed on the studio floor as an experiment, and it heavily underlines how the band truly had run its course in this original incarnation by this time.

'Swinging the Chain'

The final song on the final album recorded by the original Sabbath in the '70s—and it is sung by Bill Ward. It does appear that the track has been placed deliberately at the end, as there are signs that they knew it was all over. Lines such as 'We're so sorry, but we cannot go on in these days', together with Bill's vocal, lead one to wonder whether they knew it could not go on for another album with Ozzy, and this was a sort of goodbye. If that was the case, then it is a rather underwhelming goodbye as this is yet another song that trundles along dolefully in search of a tune. Ward struggles manfully, delivering a somewhat confused lyric that, allegedly, he wrote himself, but he really cannot rescue this. There is another nod to going 'full circle', as the harmonica in the mid-section harks back to 'The Wizard', and it does sound as if Ozzy is doing some backing vocals at the end of the song, but there is really no dressing it up: the second half of this album sounds tired and sadly uninspired, and the curtain was about to come down on the first act. The band still delivered the goods on the ensuing tour, but by the end of the year, Ozzy had played his last show with the band for the foreseeable future and it was all over. Time for a new singer to enter the stage, and enter he did.

9

Heaven and Hell

Release date: 25 April 1980
Record Label: Vertigo (UK), Warner Brothers (US)
Personnel: Ronnie James Dio, Tony Iommi, Geezer Butler, Bill
                        Ward (plus Geoff Nicholls)

A new start was clearly required following Ozzy's departure and the somewhat tired nature of some of the *Never Say Die!* material, and a new start was exactly what came about with this album. Interestingly, Ronnie James Dio was originally introduced to Iommi by Sharon Arden, who of course went on to marry Ozzy. With Dio having left Rainbow after the *Long Live Rock and Roll* album, both men were in need of new musical partners, and so, after first discussing forming an entirely new band, they decided to make it a new Black Sabbath incarnation.

   The position of bass player was initially somewhat fluid, as Geezer Butler had left temporarily while he went through a divorce, and Dio handled bass as well as vocals in the first instance, as he had on the first album by his pre-Rainbow band Elf. Demos for the album were then done with Geoff Nicholls on bass, a friend of Iommi's from Birmingham band Quartz, whose debut album Iommi had produced. When it came to actually start recording the album, ex-Rainbow bassist Craig Gruber did the honours, but when Geezer eventually returned, he redid the bass parts himself for the finished album, to finish a litany of bass players that would not disgrace the movie Spinal Tap. Nicholls also contributed some keyboards to the album, and went on to be the band's unofficial keyboard player for some years. The album was recorded between October 1979 and January 1980, in Miami and Paris, and at Dio's suggestion, they drafted in Martin Birch to handle production duties—the first time for some years that they had used an outside producer. Birch was very much from the Deep Purple 'stable', having graduated from engineer to producer with Purple, then going on to work as producer with Rainbow and Whitesnake.

There was obviously going to be a change in direction in some ways, as Dio's fantasy-oriented lyrical style marked a change, as did the fact that, for the first time, Geezer would have no lyrical involvement, since they had a singer who wrote all of his own lyrics. Iommi notes in his autobiography that his writing was also given a new lease of life by the different vocal melody style of Dio as opposed to Osbourne; Ozzy would generally tend to sing with the riff and follow the music, whereas Dio would sing across the riff and come up with opposing vocal melodies. The album was a success from the moment it was released, reaching No. 9 in the UK album chart and No. 28 in the US; yet there were some fans who staunchly maintained that the band's identity had been irrevocably changed, and that they had strayed too far from their initial blueprint—a debate that still goes on to some extent to this day. Bill Ward played on all of the album, and did the initial touring, but he was battling alcoholism at the time (later claiming he had 'no memory' of making the album), and he left during the tour to promote the album, with Vinny Appice coming in to replace him.

The famous front cover artwork was taken from a painting called *Smoking Angels* by Lynn Curlee. This was in turn originally inspired by a photograph from the 1920s of women, dressed as angels for a college pageant, smoking backstage. The rear cover featured a line drawing of the band, slightly reminiscent of the one used as the cover art for Rainbow's *Long Live Rock and Roll*. There was no gatefold sleeve nor was there an insert or inner sleeve, so all in all, the package was somewhat Spartan, which seemed a little strange for a 'grand reinvention' of sorts.

Songs

'Neon Knights'

An absolutely rampaging opener to come out of the traps and announce Dio's arrival with a bang, this is an almost perfect lead-off track. The band power along with as fast and heavy an attack as they have ever mustered, and indeed possess a lightness of touch that has rarely been evident. Dio arrives as he means to go on lyrically, with a song brimming with heroic, fantastical, and medieval metaphors, as 'protectors of the realm' do battle against 'jackals of the street', and all manner of dragons, kings, spells, and rings make an appearance. There are different ways the lyric can be interpreted, such as being an extended metaphor for love, or talking about the dichotomy of heaven *versus* hell, dealt with more explicitly elsewhere, but the important thing, and the overriding impression, is that the words suit Dio's epic vocal quality perfectly, and indeed he soars effortlessly above the band here. Surprisingly, exactly like 'Paranoid' before it, this song was the last to be written for the album, as a fast song to counterbalance the slower tracks and fill up the first side. It is also the only song on the album to actually feature songwriting input from Butler as the rest of the tracks had been fully written by the time he returned. The song was released as a single, the first from the album, and made No. 22 on the UK singles chart.

'Children of the Sea'

The first song written for the album at the very first meeting/jam between Iommi and Dio, this song had already been worked on in rudimentary form with Ozzy during the abortive sessions prior to his sacking. Indeed, Iommi claims to be in possession of a recording of a version of the track with Ozzy singing, albeit with different lyrics and melody. In any event, it turned out to be a track that Dio made his own, as he delivers an intriguing lyric, which he has commented as being about 'ecological awareness'. In that sense, it can be seen in some ways as a partner to 'Children of the Grave', only with global warming and the ozone layer replacing the atomic threat hanging over the earlier song. 'Children of the Sea' begins with a quiet, reflective opening passage until, at the end of the first verse, the band kick in with a classic Sabbath chugging riff. The chorus opens up with a more expansive melody, and around halfway through the song is an impressive instrumental section. As Iommi begins his solo, a backing choir, as of monks, accompanies him, giving the song some real gravitas and sense of the epic before the solo kicks on to another level and then plunges back to the song itself. A dramatically abrupt ending only adds to the overall effect of this superb track. A live version of this song, recorded at Deeside Leisure Centre in the UK, was used as the B-side to the 'Neon Knights' single.

'Lady Evil'

After the two classic opening tracks comes one of the lesser songs on the album. Not a bad track, but certainly one that has a somewhat perfunctory air to it. Opening with Geezer's propulsive bassline, the song, with its standard fantasy tale of a witch who puts men under her spell, comes across as more of a song to blast out with the top down in a convertible car than the typical Sabbath fare. Even the guitar solo is atypical, with its use of the wah-wah quite unusual for Iommi. It is an enjoyable, rocking track with an excellent vocal performance, but it is a way short of classic Sabbath.

'Heaven and Hell'

After the relatively slight nature of the preceding track comes what in many people's eyes is the real cornerstone of the album: its enormous title track. So key is this one song, for instance, that an excerpt from the lyric was printed proudly on the rear cover of the album. Right from the opening—a traditional big, dramatic, doomy Iommi riff—it is clear that this is classic Sabbath writ large. Dio's lyric straightaway addresses the duality of human nature, with good and evil, heaven and hell, black and white being contained within everyone. The verses are low key, propelled by Geezer's bass, before the massive chorus comes in and gives way to an even more monolithic riff afterward. The lyric is extremely accomplished, full of hidden meanings and even references the tarot at one point, with The Fool and The Dancer being mentioned ('you've got to bleed for the dancer'). Quite deep stuff. Around halfway through the track, it drops down temporarily to an expansive, almost dreamily ambient instrumental section before the pace suddenly picks up to a gallop and we are plunged headlong into the most dramatic part of the track, with Dio's impassioned, urgent vocal giving way to a marvellous guitar solo, with Iommi scattering molten gold all over the backing. It is almost all over when this breathless section grinds to a close, only for a plaintive, lone acoustic picking from Iommi draws the song to its conclusion. This track is so entwined with both Dio and Sabbath's respective musical paths that after they went their separate ways, both would retain the song regularly in their set lists, with Dio especially routinely stretching the mid-song instrumental section out with some lengthy audience participation, the nature of which would often divide opinion between elaborating on the song and losing its focus. Interestingly, it has been claimed that the iconic bassline was actually contributed by Geoff Nicholls, as it does bear some resemblance to the track 'Mainline Riders', the opening song on the debut album by his former band Quartz. All in all, probably the quintessential pairing between Dio and Sabbath, harnessing the best of both parties.

'Wishing Well'

Opening side two of the original vinyl comes this, another slightly by-the-numbers track. Again, it is not bad, and is a decent enough rock song, but there is little to lift this above the ordinary. The music is a competent, upbeat, galloping rhythm, underpinned by some admittedly excellent bass and drum work, but it does not really stick. Dio's lyric, by the same token, is very ordinary, using seemingly every cliché he is known for; not only is there a rainbow in this song, but he is also a never-ending wheel as well. Add to this one of his sometimes annoying adlibs towards the end when, among the chorus lines of him being 'your wishing well', he adds for seemingly no reason 'I wish you well', and this one is definitely on the lower tier of Dio-era Sabbath. In fact, this is a perfect illustration of the dichotomy of the Dio-Sabbath pairing—when the songs are great, they are transcendent, but when they are not so inspired, they suddenly lose everything that made Sabbath what they were and become like any other heavy rock band. Ironically, this is a perfect fit for the heaven and hell theme in a way— the magic and the mundane.

'Die Young'

Thankfully we are right back on track now, with another solid gold classic song. Dio's lyric here is fascinating, as it has been interpreted often in diametrically different ways—either as a call to 'seize the day' and live each day as if it were your last or advocating caution against that attitude and warning that the invincibility of youth is nothing more than a dangerous fantasy. Listening closely to the song and the way Dio changes his intonation at certain points, the second of those explanations seems the likelier one as the efforts to 'gather the wind' and 'chain the sun' are met with failure and disaster. Musically, while this is another fast-paced rocker (indeed, one wonders why Iommi felt he needed one more fast song when 'Neon Knights' was written), there is more going on than that. Opening with a mournful, keening lament between guitar and keyboards, the track suddenly springs into life only for it to drop down again when the first 'Tomorrow never comes' arrives from Dio. The short, reflective section then evokes the tragedy and inevitability of death, with some of Dio's most vulnerably evocative singing. As the band come back in, a brilliant Iommi solo ushers in the closing verse, chorus and run-out, as the song concludes with a lengthy fade-out. Yes, it could be argued that the song sounds more like Dio-era Rainbow than Black Sabbath, but on this occasion, it would be a churlish argument as this track is simply great, powerful, thoughtful, and intelligent rock music, and that has to be enough. The track was released as a single, backed with a live version of 'Heaven and Hell', and reached No. 41 in the UK singles chart.

'Walk Away'
Another dip here, with possibly the lowest point on the album. A somewhat uninspired Dio lyric about keeping out of a woman's clutches (there may be a deeper metaphorical meaning, but it is not sufficiently interesting to encourage the speculation this time) is married to a rather plodding and dull musical accompaniment. A song that never made it into the set list for the accompanying tour (along with 'Wishing Well'), it is easy to see why. This one does not sound like Sabbath, but it does not sound like Rainbow either. It is closer in spirit to Dio's old band Elf, though in truth it could have been done by a hundred identikit metal bands.

'Lonely is the Word'
Thankfully, another excellent track to finish on. Dio's lyric here is heartfelt, concerning a man who has had everything and lost it

all, and is expertly delivered, but this track is really all about Tony Iommi. The first couple of minutes have Dio delivering the lyrics over a grindingly heavy, yet bluesy backing, but from the point after the second and final verse, when the music drops down again, the guitar work takes over in a breathtaking three-minute display of controlled, yet grandiose soloing. If there were to be a complaint, it would be about the repetitive keyboard phrase that comes in towards the end and is so reminiscent of a part of Jimmy Page's 'Stairway to Heaven' guitar solo as to distract from Iommi's work, but it would be a shame to let that detract from what is an impressive way to finish a generally excellent album. Overall, the three tracks with the hint of filler about them and the loss of the classic Sabbath identity make this an album not quite as great in hindsight as it seemed at the time, but a stellar reinvention and rejuvenation of the band without a shadow of a doubt.

10

Mob Rules

Release date: 4 November 1981
Record Label: Vertigo (UK), Warner Brothers (US)
Personnel: Ronnie James Dio, Tony Iommi, Geezer Butler, Vinny Appice (plus Geoff Nicholls)

By the time the band came to record the follow-up to *Heaven and Hell*, Vinny Appice was thoroughly bedded in on drums, having done the second half of the preceding tour following Bill Ward's departure. He did not have a credited role in the songwriting process, however, with the songs on the album credited to Dio/Iommi/Butler, in stark contrast to all of the previous albums where credit was split four ways. For the recording, the band actually bought their own studio in Los Angeles (called 'Can Am'), and a $¼ million sound desk to go in it. This plan unravelled drastically when they went there, tried to record, and found it impossible to get a satisfactory sound anywhere in the building, even the hallway. They ended up selling the desk (and later the studio itself, which to this day is a working studio) and moved into the Record Plant once again to do the recording. The writing and recording process has been described by Dio in particular as being more difficult than that for *Heaven and Hell*, with the band dynamic starting to shift somewhat. One thing that caused some dissent at the time was reportedly the fact that Warner (US) had offered Dio a solo recording contract at the same time as Sabbath's new one, which clearly did not help the 'all for one' attitude that had s been a cornerstone of the band's working relationship in the Nevertheless, the album was a reasonable success, reaching No. 12 in the UK and No. 29 in the US.

The cover to the album was by noted fantasy artist Greg Hildebrandt, who with his brother, Tim, made up the Brothers Hildebrandt, creating artwork for many fantasy related books, games, and films in the '70s and '80s. The *Mob Rules* cover was adapted from a 1971 painting by Hildebrandt called *Dream 1: Crucifers*, which is essentially the same with the exception of the band and album names added in graffiti and some bloodstains on the floor. It has been reported that Hildebrandt himself claimed that the framework in the middle was a rack, and the skin on it was the stretched-out skin of a person. There was some controversy around the cover when it was claimed that in the added bloodstains on the floor of the painting, the word 'Ozzy' can be seen spelled out on the bottom right, or even, according to some, the words 'Kill Ozzy', with the word 'Kill' appearing in some rocks. Looking at it, it is possible to see where this is alleged to be, but Iommi dismissed these claims as 'rubbish' in his autobiography. It has also been suggested that, in the stain on the 'skin', the image of the devil's face can be made out, which, like the skin itself, is something of a stretch. Again, there was no gatefold, with the rear cover having the track names and credits against the wall background similar to the front. The early '80s were not a fertile period for expansive cover designs, but one would have thought that a band of Sabbath's stature might have had a little more clout in terms of budget than the herd.

Songs

Turn Up the Night
A hard and heavy fast-paced opener, closely following the template set by 'Neon Knights' on the previous album. It lacks the 'epic' feel and the irresistible momentum of that track, but on the other hand, it is arguably closer in spirit to the traditional Sabbath sound, with a heavier, punchier feel and more bottom end. Iommi solos quite well again, though it could be argued that he does overdo the wah-wah pedal a little, especially in the closing section of the track. Lyrically,

it is relatively straightforward and anchored in worldly concerns for Dio, as it would appear to be about being seduced by another of his mysterious, and probably evil, women. There is some mystery about exactly who or what she is, whether a succubus, witch or some other demonic being, but there are no layers of meaning which the best of his lyrics possess. The track was released as the second single from the album in 1982, and actually reached No. 24 in the US and No. 37 in the UK.

'Voodoo'

Another heavy track, with an insistent, more mid-paced riff driving it. It is a good song, with Dio's vocal melody helping to power the song along in a very symbiotic way—the riff drives the melody, the melody drives the riff. The lyrics again are reasonably straightforward, with just some need for conjecture in the matter of whose perspective the song is written from. It is clearly someone, or something, demanding service from the subject of the song, in quite a threatening manner, but whether it is intended to be God, the Devil or simply, more prosaically, some kind of actual voodoo priest is not clear. However, the truth is that it does not really matter—the impression of the powerful and controlling attitude of this being is what matters, and the effect it has on the person being addressed. There have been some claims that this lyric was actually mainly written by Geezer, but that has never been backed up with any proof, in my experience. The track was released as a single in some territories, but without any great significance—it crept to No. 46 in the US.

'The Sign of the Southern Cross'

Now this is where things get really interesting. At almost eight minutes, comfortably the longest track on the album, and also the most adventurous and grand in scope. Beginning with a quiet introductory passage, Iommi comes in with one of his most grandiose, stately riffs ever as Dio sings 'Break the crystal ball!', and from there things barely let up, shifting from quieter, reflective verses to huge choruses and even a mysterious-sounding instrumental mid-section, full of phased guitar effects and the like. The closing section of the song, with Iommi soaring over the strident, unstoppable roll of the music is one of Sabbath's great moments, making it all the more frustrating when the song begins to fade out all too soon. If ever a track was begging for a big finish, this one would be it. Still, this is overall quite an achievement, very much in the vein of the *Heaven and Hell* title track in its scope and approach. Lyrically, the song has been analysed over and over again, with increasingly elaborate explanations based on scripture, mythology, and philosophy forced onto it, but at the end of the day, it may well be, as many have suggested, simply Dio being the master of imagery, plundering various sources from fantasy, science fiction, literature, and, yes, scripture to build an intriguing set of pictures for the mind's eye to visualise and the soul to latch on to. So many questions are left unanswered: where or what is the 'small world west of wonder'? What is the significance of 'the beast'? One wonders if they were intended to be unanswered all along. The Southern Cross itself is, of course, a constellation visible only in the southern hemisphere, and as well as appearing on the flags of both Australia and New Zealand, indicating its strong significance to that part of the world, has long played a role as an evocative symbol (The Band, for example, named their 1975 album *Northern Lights – Southern Cross*), and a metaphor for an unattainable land, or a paradise, to those resident in the northern hemisphere. Ultimately, what Dio actually means is less important than the effect it has on the listener, which, like so much great music and poetry, is significant.

'E5150'

Not exactly a song, but in actuality a keyboard-driven instrumental, which sees Geoff Nicholls—not even credited as a member of the band, remember—as the dominant figure here, at least until Iommi's power chording spreads a doomy pallor over the closing half minute or so. The title is actually more interesting than the track in some ways, being a reference to 'Evil' via Roman numerals (E-5-1-50 becomes E-V-I-L when converted). As a standalone track, it does not really have tremendous merit, though it does work well as an introductory piece leading into the title track following it.

'The Mob Rules'

The (almost) title track to the album, give or take the odd definite article in the name, this song was in actual fact the first track recorded, but in different form. It was written and recorded for the soundtrack to the animated movie *Heavy Metal*, and interestingly that recording took place in Tittenhurst Park in Berkshire, the grand country house that was the former home of John Lennon and Yoko One, and immortalised in the video to the song 'Imagine' (the big white room with the piano is located in the house). The song appeared on the soundtrack album to the film, though 'E5150', also used in the film, did not. The track had to be rerecorded as the sound was so significantly different to how the rest of the album sounded, so there are two officially released yet entirely different versions of the track. Musically the song is short (just over three minutes) and to the point, with none of the grand conceits of 'Sign of the Southern Cross', either musically or lyrically. It is a track that could be said to be 'front-loaded', as it kicks in from the ashes of 'E5150' with tremendous power, and carries the first half of the song almost on pure adrenaline, before it runs slightly out of steam as the realisation sinks in that there is not much beyond that opening charge of significant note, and it has the feel of not being able to sustain anything more than its rather brief duration. Having said all that, with it carrying the title and beginning so powerfully, it does seem strange that the album was not sequenced with 'E5150' and this as the double-header opening the record and 'Turn Up the Night' closing the first side. There is a strong argument to say that 'The Mob Rules' would work much better as an opener than closer of a side of vinyl, and 'E5150' being sandwiched in the middle seems oddly misplaced. Whether the digital age removing the 'end of side' significance compounds or lessens this error is hard to judge, however. As a footnote, a shortened recording of 'E5150' was used as the intro tape music on the subsequent tour, but this then went straight into 'Neon Knights', with its erstwhile partner 'The Mob Rules' coming along much later in the set.

'Country Girl'

'Fell in love with a country girl' begins the lyric to this sprightly rocker. A country girl? Why, surely Our Ronnie has not resorted to tales of good times with farm girls behind the haystacks? No, have no fear, as she turns out immediately to be 'up from a nether world (another world?), just to bust another soul'. Ah yes, of course she was.

Never one to disappoint us, Dio here gives us a tale seemingly about a demon in human form eager to take his soul to the netherhells. As they do, of course. Unless it is another one of his many demonic metaphors that is, and just rewriting 'Evil Woman' again. In truth, it is not his most complex or opaque lyric, and is certainly not meant to be taken too seriously. Musically, it is much the same thing. A mid-tempo yet almost bouncy Iommi riff carries this along in a fairly catchy manner, with the obligatory quiet mid-section advising us to 'Sail on' again. All in all, a serviceable song, but with 'throwaway' written all over it, at least by Sabbath standards. It is quite surprising that this was passed over as a single, however.

'Slipping Away'

A rather untypical Sabbath song this one, with Iommi's riff quite good in a very Led Zeppelin-ish way (a riff that would fit like a glove onto *Physical Graffiti*), and Geezer Butler also producing some great bass work. They work admirably together on this, but it is rather an example of a riff in search of a song as Dio labours to attempt to fashion a melody where one hardly exists, with a rather dull lyric about a guy always having to be on the move and leave his woman and home behind for a new place, etc. It is been done hundreds of times, from the Allman Brothers' 'Ramblin' Man' downward, and this is not one of the best. The instrumental section in the middle is something of a muddled mess, and one gets the impression that, if there had been much in the way of extra material, this one might not have made the cut. Definite filler.

'Falling Off the Edge of the World'

Much more substance to this one. Dio's lyric is quite a thoughtful and poignant one about a man who feels his life is slipping away from him, with the first verses hinting that he may be contemplating suicide owing to the fact that he has never been allowed to reach his potential in the world and his hope has evaporated. It begins beautifully, with Dio wringing every bit of sadness and hopelessness out of those first verses as one is led to believe the song is going to be a ballad of sorts. A slow yet majestically grandiose section follows before the main passage of the song kicks in with a fast riff at the two-minute mark. From there, it is a breakneck race to the finish line, with the galloping nature of the track together with Dio's vocal heavily foreshadowing what Iron Maiden would begin perfecting the following year with the *Number of the Beast* album. Musically, it is good, fast, and powerful, with an impressive double-tracked guitar solo, but overall, there is the impression of the potential of the first two minutes not really being lived up to. Played slightly less safe, with a few more twists and turns, this could have been a real classic. As it is, even with its faults, it is still among the best moments on the album.

'Over and Over'

An album closer that is inescapably from the same mould as 'Lonely Is the Word' from the previous album, this slow, heavy, bluesy lament has a similar lyrical theme of melancholy to that former track, with Dio lamenting the fact that his pain and despair are at such an unbearable level that he is incapable even of feeling empathy for the fate of others any more as his anguish simply goes on 'over and over and over again'. Some have even speculated that it could be an ecological song, with the central character actually being the earth itself, mourning what has become of it, though that may possibly be something of a leap. It is a powerfully delivered song, with Dio on good form, and filled with two separate passages of incendiary soloing from Iommi, but the impression left is partially one of *déjà vu* as the template is so close to the aforementioned 'Lonely Is the Word'—with both songs closing their respective albums—that its impact is blunted. Indeed, a criticism that could be levelled at the album as a whole, with the best tracks on that previous album having such clear links here ('Neon Knights' is 'Turn Up the Night', 'Heaven and Hell' is 'Sign of the Southern Cross', etc.), is that *Mob Rules* is something of a retread of its predecessor. While it may not be a much worse album track for track, there was a sense of reinvention and an exciting new dawn about the release of *Heaven and Hell* that made its faults easier to overlook in the grand scheme of things, which here is missing. It was, in retrospect, perhaps time for a change again before the band began once again going through the motions, and after the live album *Live Evil*, change there certainly was. Though the form in which it arrived would not be what many would have expected, nor were they all happy about it by any means.

11

Born Again

Release date: 7 August 1983 (UK), 4 October 1983 (US)
Record Label: Vertigo (UK), Warner Brothers (US)
Personnel: Ian Gillan, Tony Iommi, Geezer Butler, Bill Ward
(plus Geoff Nicholls)

With the *Mob Rules* line-up having dissolved amid accusations of covert remixing during work on the *Live Evil* album, Tony Iommi had resolved to retire the Black Sabbath name. He had switched management to Don Arden (father of Ozzy's future wife, Sharon, of course), and he initially had vague plans to form a new 'supergroup' project, when Arden stepped in and insisted on them using the Sabbath name so—with Geezer and the returning, and newly sober, Bill Ward on board—that was how it was to be. Several singers were considered (including, bizarrely, an audition tape from a young Michael Bolton) before Ian Gillan was settled on, and another Black Sabbath was born—or born again, to be precise. The band set about recording the album in May 1983 at Richard Branson's manor Studios in Oxford, with the band living in the grand house in which they were situated—all except for Gillan, who bizarrely opted to live in a large marquee tent outside, claiming it to be better for his voice. The album did extremely well in the UK, reaching No. 4 in the album charts, though it only reached No. 39 in the US, indicating perhaps a greater scepticism about the project. The album received generally dreadful reviews and, despite the good sales, it has been regularly dismissed over the years by many fans, while the subsequent tour, which saw the band include Deep Purple's 'Smoke on the Water' in the set, certainly did not help the line-up's credibility. Iommi has since commented that while Gillan had a superb voice, he was totally incompatible with Sabbath—a view held equally by Gillan himself, who has said he felt uncomfortable with performing the old Sabbath material live. When the band heard the album, while they were away touring, they were aghast at the muddy production quality (courtesy of Robin Black, and allegedly due to equipment issues), but it was too late to change it.

If there had been controversy and criticism around the *Sabotage* and *Technical Ecstasy* covers, it was nothing compared to what greeted this one. Featuring a garishly coloured red 'devil baby', complete with horns, claws and fangs, against a hideously clashing blue background, it was loathed by Gillan and Ward, and has regularly featured in lists of the worst rock album covers ever produced. Iommi clearly must have liked it, as he approved it, but he certainly found himself in a stark minority. In actual fact, the image was based on a photo of a baby from the cover of a 1968 partwork-encyclopedia/magazine called *Mind Alive*, which the cover artist Steve Joule's parents had bought him as a child. The same photo was also used as the basis for the cover of Depeche Mode's single 'New Life', which as a result looks startlingly similar to the Sabbath cover, only without the horns, claws, etc. (or ghastly red colour). The back cover was better, featuring round photographs of the four musicians, with the song titles and credits in red and yellow gothic font against a black background, but it was too little to rescue the package. One nice touch was the prominent credit for the keyboards of Geoff Nicholls, even if he still was not listed as a band member.

Songs

'Trashed'

It would be difficult to imagine a greater contrast immediately to Dio or Butler's epic or scholarly lyrics as Gillan penned this opening track about an incident when he returned from the local pub the worse for wear (allegedly travelling back via the canal in an inflatable dinghy) and decided to take Bill Ward's new car for a spin around the manor's go-kart track. The car was wrecked when he hit a tyre, flipped over, and landed upside down and trapped just short of the swimming pool. He claims that he believed the car was his, but this did not stop the furious Ward taking revenge by way of Gillan's boat. The 'Peter and the Greenfly' referenced in the lyric are Iommi's guitar tech Peter Resty and manor gardener Ian, known as 'Greenfly', who witnessed the incident. A long way from 'The Sign of the Southern Cross'. Musically, the song is pretty much a match for the lyrics, being a straight ahead up-tempo rocker—not bad in its way, but really having far more in common with Gillan's own eponymous band, which had recently folded, than with Black Sabbath. The track was released as a single and was even accompanied by a hilariously dreadful video. Unsurprisingly, it did not chart, even with the added publicity of being included on the famed 'Filthy Fifteen' list by the PMRC, based on its apparently glorifying drinking and driving. All in all, things had now become closer in spirit to 'Carry On Screaming' than 'The Devil Rides Out'.

'Stonehenge'

Like 'E5150' on the *Mob Rules* album, this short two-minute track is an almost ambient keyboard-based instrumental serving in effect as two minutes of filler to lead into the following track, 'Disturbing the Priest'. An extended, double-length version of this track was used as the B-side to the 'Trashed' single, and later included on CD copies of the album as a bonus track. Similar to 'E5150', however, it is perhaps chiefly notable for its title, presaging, and allegedly inspiring, the band's legendary plan to have a replica of Stonehenge built as a stage prop for the tour. In a move directly inspiring the famous Spinal Tap sequence, Geezer had jotted down the design for the people who were to produce it, but when it arrived, it was so enormous that it would not fit in the venues. He had written the dimensions down in centimetres, the designers had read it as inches, and it came back almost the size of the actual Stonehenge. In the end, only a small amount of the massive stones was used.

'Disturbing the Priest'

Coming in dramatically from the end of the meandering 'Stonehenge', this turned out to be one of the most popular pieces on the album.

again inspired from a real-life incident: in this case, after the use of rehearsal space in a building near a local church resulted in complaints from the resident clergy. Gillan had the idea for the phrase 'We're disturbing the priest', and then wrote this lyric about the eternal struggle between good and evil. The opening section of the song is one of Iommi's most evil and menacing sounding riffs for several years, and Gillan's vocals, and demonic laughter, sound positively unhinged. Certainly an arresting opening, though the track as a whole does once again begin to lose its focus a little as it starts to meander in a slightly directionless way from passage to passage. More ambitious than most of the album, certainly, but not entirely in a positive way. Decent effort at the old Sabbath spirit, though.

'The Dark'

Yet another space-filling instrumental leading into 'Zero the Hero', only this time, it is even more inconsequential as it is only forty-five seconds of supposedly menacing sound. They were starting to use this trick a little too often at this point. Still, at least it does bring us to the next track.

'Zero the Hero'

Almost certainly the best track on the album, as well as the longest at around seven and a half minutes, 'Zero the Hero' sees Gillan directing withering scorn at a privileged man who he regards as a complete loser despite everything being made so easy for him. It has some echoes of Dylan's 'Like a Rolling Stone' in that regard and makes for an interesting lyric. There are some odd moments, such as the bizarre rhyming of 'sit by the river' with 'they eat raw liver', and Gillan's frankly surreal invention of the word 'impissibolity', but none of this affects proceedings when listening to it. Opening with a huge, heavy introductory section presaging Metallica's 'Enter Sandman' by several years, the song settles into an easy, rolling, yet somehow darkly menacing riff that insinuates its way into the listener's brain. Gillan delivers the verses in particular in a half-talking style, which is a foreshadowing of the approach taken by rap artists later, and actually works extremely well in conjunction with that constant, thrumming riff behind it. The best part of the track, however, is the mid-song instrumental section, which sees Iommi soloing over the repetitive, insistent throb of that riff in spectacularly effective style, all the more so for the fact that he makes it sound as if it is completely effortless and he is nonchalantly avoiding any dramatic clichés, whereas to produce that effect, it has to be extremely cleverly written. This is much more of the direction the band should have gone in than the vapid banality of the likes of 'Trashed', as they succeed in updating the old Sabbath drone and creating a whole new template. Many have pointed out the close similarity between that main riff and, in sped up form, Guns and Roses' much later 'Paradise City'—indeed, it is easy to see why. What is also inconclusive is whether Gillan got the idea for the title from the Gong track of a few years earlier called 'Zero the Hero and The Witch's Spell', but it surely must be a possibility that it was at least in his subconscious. Great way to finish the original first side of vinyl, though. The second side would struggle to match it.

'Digital Bitch'
The lyric to this musically slight fast rocker of a track is ironically not far removed from the much more intense 'Zero the Hero', though taken in a more light-hearted way. It concerns a daughter of a rich businessman who lives her life for pleasure and treats those who she deems 'beneath her' with disdain, and the tongue-in-cheek approach of Gillan can be seen in the rhyming of 'a fortune from computers' with 'a greedy emotional looter' and, worse still, his use of the word 'ginormous'. A cynic might say that never have so many yearned for Dio to come in warbling about his 'rainbows' again. The song has long been strongly rumoured to be about Sharon Osbourne, but Gillan has never revealed the truth about this, only commenting that neither the subject in question nor her father had anything to do with computers, and that was only in there to facilitate the rhyme. It may well be that the Osbourne/Arden connection is merely a convenient retrofit of the lyric after the event as there is no evidence to support it. Musically, the track is enjoyable enough, barrelling away at an extremely lively pace, but it lacks depth. Certainly not the worst song on the album, though.

'Born Again'
The title track to the album is also the most unexpected, containing as it does an excellent Gillan lyric, alluding obliquely to the darkness

and conflict within his soul and the questions of hope and rebirth. Musically, it takes the form of a big, slow-paced 'power ballad', with Gillan emoting powerfully in the dramatic chorus. However, despite all of these excellent ingredients, the track somehow disappoints ultimately as somewhat less than the sum of its parts. The guitar accompaniment to the verses is repetitive and not really strong enough to carry such repetition, and it ends up becoming somewhat dull as it progresses, with Gillan's vocal work in the verses calling to mind Deep Purple's 'When a Blind Man Cries', only not as effective or atmospheric. One of the problems here, and indeed on much of the album, is that the vocal melodies are simply not as strong as Dio's or even Ozzy's, and rarely become memorable. Almost as a representation of the album in microcosm, the title track comes and goes with everything sounding quite good, while somehow failing to capture the magic. Not bad, but not great—and that is not enough.

'Hot Line'

Once again, this grindingly heavy mid-to-up-tempo song sees Gillan struggling manfully for a memorable vocal melody, and once again finds it wanting. This is all the more damaging to this particular track as the music takes it into the territory of Purple's 'Woman from Tokyo' or Rainbow's 'All Night Long', which leaves it by association crying out for a big, hook-laden vocal delivery, but it is a struggle to remember the track after it has played. The lyric is a fairly slight one again, with Gillan taking the part of a loser needing help when he repeatedly falls, and is not helped by his use of the word 'baby', which is really anathema to the spirit of the Black Sabbath we have come to know and love. Probably the weakest song on the album (instrumentals excepted), nudging out 'Trashed'.

'Keep It Warm'

A slightly better approach to the melody side of things on this closing song, which begins as a sort of anthemic, 'scarf-waving' track with the chorus actually managing to be memorable and encouraging the listener to sing along with it as it gets bigger and bigger. There is also a switch to a faster tempo in the excellent mid-song instrumental section, with the ever-reliable Iommi soloing as well as ever, before the main body of the song returns to bring the album to a close with a long, repetitive build of that big chorus, almost ending on a 'feel-good' note, which is not the emotion one would generally expect at the end of a Sabbath album. Gillan's lyrics are unapologetic generic tosh about him having to leave his woman (he is 'a gypsy', of course—they always seem to be), but that he will be coming back to her (presumably, the gypsy in his soul only needs to be taken out for the odd trip here and there); in the end, it does not matter as the feel of the track is what is important, and in this case, it is big, comforting, and warm. A good closer to an album that is perhaps not as bad as some of its detractors (who are many) would have you believe, but certainly not the unsung classic that the other extreme of the fan base would claim either. It has its moments, but it does rank toward the bottom end of Black Sabbath's albums. Not the very bottom, however, which we will come onto. This line-up splintered after this one album, with Bill Ward's relapse into drinking after a long sober period forcing his withdrawal and return to America before the tour even began, for which former Move and ELO man Bev Bevan stood in. After that tour, they would shatter completely.

12

The Seventh Star

Release date: 28 January 1986 (Credited to 'Black Sabbath Featuring
                Tony Iommi')
Record Label: Vertigo (UK), Warner Brothers (US)
Personnel: Tony Iommi, Glenn Hughes, Dave Spitz, Eric Singer,
                Geoff Nicholls

After the *Born Again* line-up splintered following the tour supporting
the album, with even the loyal Butler stepping down to devote more
time to his family, Tony Iommi was left as the sole Sabbath member
left standing and in full control of the name. Feeling utterly weary
with getting the Black Sabbath 'machine' up and running again and
again, he decided that the time was right to finally retire the name
and record a solo album. To this effect, he gathered around him some
big names (his fellow Midlander Glenn Hughes on vocals, though
oddly enough not handling bass duties) and some less so (then-
unknown future Kiss drummer Eric Singer and bass player Dave
Spitz) alongside Geoff Nicholls, and set about recording the album
that would become *The Seventh Star*. The album (produced by noted
ex-Kansas producer Jeff Glixman) was recorded and finished when
US label Warner Bros began to get cold feet about the commercial
potential of the album, and, together with Don Arden, pushed Iommi
to make it a Black Sabbath record. He was very reluctant to do so, but
eventually agreed to the compromise, which saw the album credited
to 'Black Sabbath Featuring Tony Iommi', a clumsy halfway-house

that alienated many. The musical style was understandably different to the Sabbath template—indeed intentionally so—and the use of the band name saw the record compared unfavourably, and perhaps unfairly, with the band's previous output. It was not exactly what would be called classic even on its own terms, but that association was not kind to it.

Like the music contained within, the cover photo of the album, featuring a fringed leather jacket-wearing Iommi looking somewhat wistful against a bare desert landscape, would have worked much better adorning a solo record. Likewise, the back cover with another, similar photo completing a rather drab package, which made a mockery of the Sabbath name by not featuring the rest of the band at all. Still, it did at least come with a nicely designed inner sleeve including the lyrics and a slightly disturbing illustration by German painter Cranach the Elder, which was a bonus at least.

Songs

'In for the Kill'

An adrenaline-fuelled, fast-paced opener, this follows the template set on every recent album since *Heaven and Hell*, but it actually does it very well. With epic, heroic swords-and-chariots lyrics surprisingly well sung by Glenn Hughes (since they are way out of his usual comfort zone), this is an extremely good power-metal track and does a great job of opening the album. Iommi's solo is fast, furious, and top-quality, and there is not really a wasted moment on this breathlessly impulsive track. A great start, but not really representative of the album as a whole.

'No Stranger to Love'

A completely different direction here, as the band, perhaps unwisely, elect to follow the prevailing trend and attempt a big-hair, big-production, overwrought '80s power ballad. This is one of the tracks where the use of the Sabbath name was particularly detrimental as, taken on its own merits, this is not a bad song: Iommi wrings every last bit of emotion he can from his solo, while Glenn Hughes shows how strong his voice really can be. Unfortunately, however, when

Above left: Ozzy's family home at 14 Lodge Road, Aston. A very typical Victorian working-class terrace. (*Photo by Stephen Lambe*)

Above right: Geezer's old house (the grey one), Friar Park Villas. Only slightly grander than Ozzy's. (*Photo by Stephen Lambe*)

Below: Newtown Community Centre, Aston. Sabbath's first rehearsal hall, very near to Ozzy and Geezer. (*Photo by Stephen Lambe*)

Above: The first two albums, with original inner gatefolds. (*Original Vertigo pressings*)

Below: *Master of Reality*, original Vertigo issue with flip-top cover.
(*Author's collection; original photo by Chris Walkden*)

Above: *Volume 4*, original gatefold booklet—outer view.
(*Author's collection; original photo by Chris Walkden*)

Below: *Volume 4*, original gatefold booklet—inner view.
(*Author's collection; original photo by Chris Walkden*)

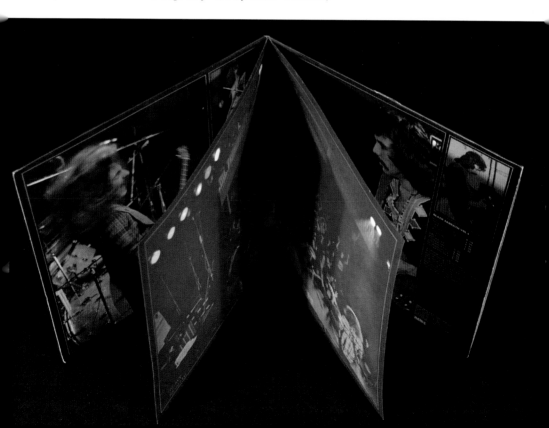

Above: *Sabbath Bloody Sabbath*, original UK gatefold.
(*Author's collection; original photo by Chris Walkden*)

Below *Sabbath Bloody Sabbath*, original UK inner gatefold and inner sleeve.
(*Author's collection; original photo by Chris Walkden*)

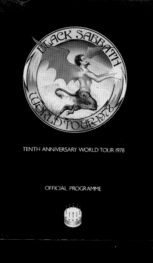
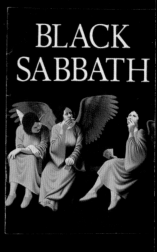

Above: UK tour programmes, 1977, 1978, and 1979.
(*Author's collection; original photo by Chris Walkden*)

Below: Spread from 1977 programme, with custom cartoons.
(*Author's collection; original photo by Chris Walkden*)

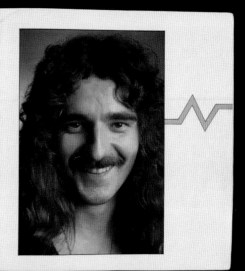

Above: Inner spread from 1978 tenth-anniversary UK tour programme. Note the birthday cake. (*Author's collection; original photo by Chris Walkden*)

Below: Another spread from 1978 tour programme, and more birthday cake pictures. (*Author's collection; original photo by Chris Walkden*)

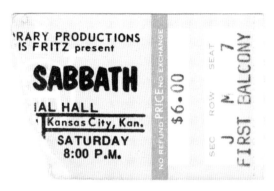

Above: Concert ticket stubs from 1976 and 1978, Kansas, US. (*Photo by Jim Collins*)

Below: Inner spread from 1980 *Heaven and Hell* UK tour programme, first leg. (*Author's collection; original photo by Chris Walkden*)

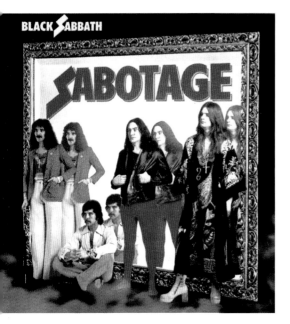

Above left: The oft-maligned *Sabotage* front. (*Sanctuary Records/NEMS*)

Above right: *Technical Ecstasy* front cover, with its bizarre image. (*Sanctuary Records/Vertigo*)

Below: The concert attire of choice, *c.* early 1980s. (*Author's collection; original photo by Chris Walkden*)

Above: *Born Again* picture disc. (*Photo by Diego Torres Silvestre*)

Below: *Born Again* picture disc, reverse side. (*Photo by Diego Torres Silvestre*)

Above left: *Heaven and Hell* front cover. (*Sanctuary Records/Vertigo*)

Above right: *Heaven and Hell* back cover. (*Sanctuary Records/Vertigo*)

Below: *Mob Rules* front cover, with so-called 'Kill Ozzy' message in bottom right. (*Sanctuary Records/Vertigo*)

Above: *The Eternal Idol*: Tony Martin's debut album with the band. (*Sanctuary Records/Vertigo*)

Below: Bev Bevan and Tony Iommi with guitarist Gordon Giltrap, recording session for Shadows tribute album *Twang!*, 1996. (*Photo courtesy Gordon Giltrap*)

Black Sabbath comic, published 1994 by Rock-It Comics. (*Photo by Jennifer Rogers*)

Above: Ronnie James Dio's memorial, Hollywood Hills Cemetery, Los Angeles.
(*Photo by Paul Brown*)

Below: Tony Iommi pictured at an exhibition of Sabbath memorabilia, Birmingham.
(*Photo courtesy Birmingham City Council*)

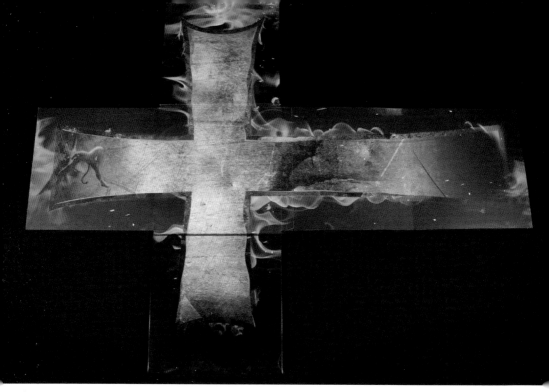

Above: The magnificent 'flaming cross' packaging of *The Ultimate Collection* compilation, BMG Records. (*Author's collection; original photo by Chris Walkden*)

Below: The reverse of that same compilation, with the four discs showing scale. (*Author's collection; original photo by Chris Walkden*)

Above and below: On stage in Manchester, January 2017, 'The End' tour, final leg. (*Photo by Daniel Robinson*)

Above and below: On stage in Manchester, January 2017, 'The End' tour, final leg. (*Photo by Daniel Robinson*)

taken as a Black Sabbath song, this comes across as totally wrong and out of step. A dreadful promo video of the song, featuring *Star Trek: The Next Generation* actress Denise Crosby, a random and seemingly irrelevant dog, a beard-and-mullet sporting Hughes, and a hopelessly miscast moody Iommi, did not really help matters. Not bad by any means and, ironically, given the presence of Hughes, a great fit for late 1980s Whitesnake. All wrong to be associated with Sabbath, though. The bass here is by Gordon Copley, who began the recording before being replaced by Spitz.

'Turn to Stone'
Back to the power metal here, mining the same vein as 'In for the Kill', but markedly less successfully. It is unclear who wrote which lyrics on this album as all lyrics are credited collectively (although rumour has it that Geoff Nicholls wrote much of the lyrical content), but Hughes sounds rather uncomfortable trying to wrap his larynx around this clichéd tale of the hoary old dangerous woman with a demon in her soul, up from hell to get you, no escape, and so on. The riff itself is okay, and it powers things along quite well, but there is no hook and little melody for Hughes to get his teeth into. It is not terrible, but it basically comes, hangs around for three or four minutes, and closes the door on its way out. Disposable.

'Sphinx (The Guardian)'
Here we have yet another of those short keyboard instrumentals/song intros that Sabbath albums of this time had become infested with. It is fine for what it is—all long, held, atmospheric chords—but it really has no business being a separately credited song. It would be understandable if it was credited to Nicholls, and gave him a songwriting nod, but it is not and it does not. Still, it does what it is there for, and it sets up for the next track.

'The Seventh Star'
The title track of the album, and easily the most lyrically interesting, with all manner of pyramid and sand imagery placing us firmly in ancient Egypt for this well-written tableau of fallen angels, God's judgement, and the mysterious 'call of the seventh star'. All very Dio-esque, in fact—and in a decidedly good way. Musically, it

attempts to conjure up the matching epic atmosphere, with an insistent mid-tempo marching riff accompanied at times by monk-like chanting backing vocals. Iommi conjures up some appropriately 'Eastern-sounding' solo licks a little reminiscent of Rainbow's classic 'Stargazer'. Frustratingly, it does not quite take off, lacking a properly grandiose climax, and, try as he might, Hughes just is not the right vocalist for this. Still, it is a good effort, worthy of much praise for ambition and is certainly well worthy of the Sabbath name. 'Turn to Stone' apart, it closes a pretty decent first side of vinyl.

'Danger Zone'

Another fairly up-tempo rocker here, driven along by a superb throbbing, circular riff from Iommi. Indeed, so infectious is the riff that it almost makes up for the fact that there is not too much a song written around it. Almost, but not quite, as what this is crying out for is a great chorus that stands proud before launching us back into the great rhythm of that riff, but that does not happen as, once again, the vocal melody is weak. A somewhat perfunctory guitar solo and a rather dull lyric rehashing 'Life in the Fast Lane' (but worse) or 'Living After Midnight' (thankfully better) leave this one starting out extremely promisingly, but outstaying its welcome long before its four-and-a-half-minute duration. 'A' for effort, but 'C' for content here.

'Heart Like a Wheel'

A lengthy blues workout, this is a prime example of why this album should never have been credited to Sabbath. As a Tony Iommi solo record, this sees him stretching out in a new direction, and enjoying the unusual luxury of blues scale soloing, but representing Black Sabbath this is all wrong. Lyrically, it is wall-to-wall clichés (the woman has a heart like a wheel, ready to roll away from the despairing Hughes, out on the road etc., while he is 'left standing here'), but then again, as a blues song, it is not only acceptable, but quite probably even intentional. The scenery-chewing vocals are all part of the same package. For what it is, it is quite good. It has a lazy groove, the guitar work is splendid, and the vocals emote heavily throughout. As an actual song, it is very simple and does not have much in the way of substance.

'Angry Heart'

Much better songwriting here as this is a genuinely catchy, yet cleverly constructed piece. It opens with what seems like a standard chugging riff, but after each verse, it opens out into a great ascending and descending guitar figure that not only keeps the song interesting, but gives Hughes' vocal somewhere to go at the end of the line. Altogether, it just works, even if it does have as much of a Deep Purple feel to it as a Black Sabbath one. Interesting lyrics as well, ostensibly about a man who is destroying his chance of happiness by the anger and bitterness he carries within him, but it leaves the resolution open-ended as he seems to accept his problem and makes the listener speculate as to whether he has resolved it and bought himself some peace in his soul. One of the best tracks on the album.

'In Memory'

Coming straight in from the end of 'Angry Heart', this short, two-and-a-half-minute ballad is curiously insubstantial for an album closer as it really does not go anywhere and, again, leaves Hughes to try to wring the emotion out of an undistinguished melody. The heartfelt words were reportedly written by Geoff Nicholls following the death of his mother, but they really deserve better. There is not even a solo of note as the song fades out just as it appears it may get going, rather than a big climax as on 'Lonely Is the Word', which is all the more perplexing as, at only thirty-five minutes, this is quite a short album.

All told, as mentioned before, this is a perfectly acceptable Tony Iommi solo record, as indeed it should have been. As a Black Sabbath album, it is a complete failure, and that is a shame. The next album would see the 'Sabbath Brand' begin to reassert itself, however.

13

The Eternal Idol

Release date: 23 November 1987
Record Label: Vertigo (UK), Warner Brothers (US)
Personnel: Tony Iommi, Tony Martin, Eric Singer, Bob Daisley,
              Geoff Nicholls

The gestation of this album was confusing to say the least. Glenn Hughes had been fired from *The Seventh Star* tour after only five dates owing to his substance-aggravated unreliability, with Ray Gillen coming in to replace him. This hiring of another singer named Gillen (despite different spelling) led to more confusion, as can be imagined. The deluxe version of *The Seventh Star* includes a Hammersmith show from the tour, and it is less than great to say the least. When the tour finished, the line-up—now confirmed as 'Black Sabbath' officially—reconvened in Air Studio in Montserrat to start work on what became this album. Dave Spitz, however, quit almost immediately to be replaced by Bob Daisley who had interestingly played with Dio in Rainbow and also in Ozzy's band. For some reason, Spitz is credited on the sleeve, but in fact, Daisley handled all of the bass on the album. After initial sessions there produced some recordings, the band returned to London to finish the album at Battery Studios, at which time Gillen departed to be replaced by Tony Martin. This was to be a significant step on the road to a more settled band, as Martin would eventually appear on four more albums after this one, making him the longest serving Sabbath vocalist after Ozzy. Bev Bevan is credited with percussion on the sleeve, but this was in fact no more than some cymbal overdubs and the like on one or two tracks after Singer and Daisley had also departed by the end of recording. The 2010 deluxe edition of the album contains the original Montserrat sessions with Ray Gillen on vocals. The album was, unsurprisingly after the recent upheavals, a poor seller, only reaching No. 66 in the UK and a lowly No. 168 in the US. It was, however, much better than that, and history has been kind to the record. The album was produced by, at various times, Jeff Glixman, Chris Tsangardes, and Vic Coppersmith-Heaven.

The front cover was intended to feature a Rodin statue that was actually called *The Eternal Idol*. However, typical of the chaos surrounding Sabbath at this time, permission to use the statue was refused and they ended up getting two models, painted head to foot, posing to recreate the statue. To make matters worse, the all-over paint had some toxic effects that Iommi believes may have entailed them requiring hospital treatment after the shoot. This echoed an earlier mishap when Bill Ward suffered the same fate after he was painted head to toe, naked, during the anarchic *Volume 4* sessions, with no skin left unpainted to breathe, but that time they at least had youth and vast quantities of drugs to excuse the incident. The back cover was just a plain black background with the song titles and credits on it, but there was an inner sleeve featuring the lyrics. It is not a great package, however.

Songs

'The Shining'

Any fears that this was going to be another false start are banished immediately as 'The Shining' leaps from the speakers. A genuine Sabbath classic, a low-key opening soon gives way to a trademark Iommi loping riff before new man Tony Martin completes the picture, his confident vocal so reminiscent of Dio that at first one does a double-take. By the time the chorus comes in, we are sold, as Martin's strident 'Rise up! To the shining' elevates the track higher than any since the Dio glory days. Iommi's guitar work is exceptional as ever, and overall the track manages the twin trick of sounding faithful to the original Sabbath spirit, and yet also leaving one punching the air and singing along. Not an easy balance to maintain, as the previous couple of albums have made clear. The song is almost six minutes in length, yet seems to be over in half that time, such is its irresistible feel. The lyric certainly appears to be inspired by the Stephen King book of the same name, with its references to 'the house' haunting the characters, the 'shining' giving rise to visions, and the 'house on the hill' leading to insanity. The song was released as a single, with Tony Martin-penned track 'Some Kind of Woman' on the B-side, but it failed to bother the charts, scandalously. A video for the track was filmed in chaotic circumstances, when, with Daisley having left and the band having no bassist at the time, an unknown guitarist was dragged in off the street to play the part of the bassist for the film. His name, alas, is lost to history. The drummer in the video is ex-Clash man Terry Chimes (memorably credited as 'Tory Crimes' on the debut Clash album) as he was at the time standing in for tour drummer Bev Bevan. Needless to say, the video is eminently disposable, if not exactly 'forgettable', for the farcical reasons above.

'Ancient Warrior'
Another doomy, plodding Iommi riff promises great things here, but the song falls short of the opener. The verses struggle to weave a melody around the riff, and Martin sounds a little ill at ease here. The chorus, when it arrives, is better and lifts the song significantly, and the guitar solo is first rate, with a little more of that classic 'Stargazer' sound incorporated, but overall, the impression is of a song trying a little too hard, other than that admittedly great chorus. The lyrics are interesting, telling a tale of the titular ancient warrior seemingly doomed to never be able to put a stop to the fighting and death. Many have interpreted the song as being specifically about Jesus Christ, or even, from another viewpoint, Lucifer, but Daisley has claimed that it was not in fact about any particular figure, but in reality, a—possibly allegorical—fictional character.

'Hard Life to Love'
A much more upbeat track here, with none of the gravitas shown on the previous two songs. It is not exactly poor; indeed, on the contrary, it is a catchy enough heavy rock song, but the fact remains that it

does sound as if it would be much more at home on a Whitesnake album. Unlike *The Seventh Star*, this album was intended to represent the name Black Sabbath right from the start, and this does not really do it. The lyric is quite interesting, relating to a man trying to distance himself from what he perceives as wrong with the world, but the music brings none of that out, and gives the song a much more 'throwaway' feel than it deserves. One point of interest: two places in the song when Iommi appears to briefly channel the chugging riff from the Heart song 'Barracuda'—to good effect, I may add. Overall, though, unremarkable.

'Glory Ride'

Back on the 'epic' trail now, as this superbly strident track allows Martin's voice free rein to soar above the music, with a suitably triumphant guitar solo taking nothing away from this majesty. The lyric would appear to be very possibly in reference to the Battle of Britain, with its talk of the heroes in the sky where eagles dare, facing the enemy's gun, etc., the fate of a nation in their hands, and taking their hero's bow come the morning. It is possible that what is being described is some fantasy tale of mythical flying warriors, but the reference to the 'enemy's gun' would seem to be a jarring anachronism were that to be the case. Whatever the intent, it is a stirring and stunning track, in equal measure, bringing the original first vinyl side to a triumphant end.

'Born to Lose'

Another fairly generic, single-minded up-tempo rocker. Once again, the song rides on a nice Iommi motoring riff (he never lost his knack for 'The Riff'), but there is very little else going on beneath the surface. The lyric is from the point of view of someone who is 'the worm that turned', vowing to get one over at last on whoever has wronged him. There is not a lot of subtlety, but to give it credit, it is possible to see how someone who has been the victim of bullying or abuse could find it empowering, so from that point of view, it is a creditable message. Martin here ends up sounding like Klaus Meine from the Scorpions at times—one thing that is clear from this album is that, great voice notwithstanding, he has yet to find his own identity as a vocalist. That would come soon enough, however.

'Nightmare'

A nice dramatic change of pace here, with a track beginning as an old-school Sabbath chugger before going into an up-tempo midsection and back again. It is not classic, but it is pretty good. In fact, the song was born out of Tony Iommi being asked to do the music for the film *A Nightmare on Elm Street.* The plan fell through, much to Iommi's disappointment, over money issues (old manager Patrick Meehan had bizarrely been hired once again to replace Don Arden in a move that Iommi expressed profound regret about in his autobiography, and had apparently priced them out of the job), but he had already written a song for the abortive soundtrack and it became this one. The lyric has all of the old touchstones such as the Devil, the Reaper, visions with wings, an evil spirit, and an equally evil pit—not to be taken seriously, but a welcome nod to the past. One of the better tracks on the album, if a step below 'The Shining' or 'Glory Ride'. The demonic laughter heard midway through was actually provided by Ray Gillen, oddly enough the only contribution from him that was left in place.

'Scarlet Pimpernel'

Another one of those darned instrumental intros credited as a separate track, though this one is at least an Iommi guitar piece that harks back to 'Orchid' and the like. It is quite nice, and clocks in at just over two minutes, so can perhaps be counted as more than a mere intro to 'Lost Forever'.

'Lost Forever'

Another very strong track. The central riff is a fast, yet powerful propulsive monster, while the insistent, hammering middle eight is even more so. Telling the tale of a man facing the hangman's noose and looking back over his past misdeeds and lack of forgiveness, the lyrics also have the right feel to marry up with the music. The album is building to a strong end by this time.

'Eternal Idol'

Nowhere is this strong ending more apparent than in the form of this six-and-a-half-minute title piece. Touching on the old Sabbath theme of Christ's ability to defeat the forces of evil, it is probably the most 'vintage Sabbath' track on the album. Beginning with a sledgehammer-heavy, slow grinding intro, it soon drops down to a quiet verse section clearly inspired by the song 'Black Sabbath' itself, as is the huge chorus. In fact, 'Black Sabbath' is what impresses as the clearest inspiration of this song. There is even a slight suggestion of the old 'Monk's Chorus' at one point during the mid-song instrumental. It is not anywhere near as good as that timeless old classic, of course, but along with 'The Shining' and 'Glory Ride', it is probably fair to say this forms part of the album's 'triple crown'. Martin would start to sound much more confident in his identity in the next album, and progress would continue.

Related Song

'Some Kind of Woman'

The final song written, and the first composed with Tony Martin, appeared as the B-side to the single 'The Shining'. It once again sees the chameleon-like performance on this album nudge into Deep Purple territory, and it really is a throwaway fast rocker. The song finally appeared on album as a bonus track on later CD versions of the album, and a host of Sabbath fans collectively shook their heads and wondered what the fuss was about, but then again, it was never a song intending to change the world, just to bring Tony Martin into the songwriters' collective. That was a move that would pay big dividends quite soon down the line. As the band began touring the album, chaos yet again ensued, with Eric Singer following Spitz out of the band, and clash drummer Terry Chimes coming in on a temporary basis, only to be replaced again by Bev Bevan.

14

Headless Cross

Release date: 24 April 1989
Record Label: IRS
Personnel: Tony Iommi, Tony Martin, Geoff Nicholls, Cozy
              Powell (plus Laurence Cottle)

Before the recording of this album, the band had been dropped by both Warner in the US and Vertigo in the UK, and so found themselves in the unusual position of looking for a record deal. Miles Copeland, former manager of Wishbone Ash, Gordon Giltrap, and The Police, among others, and elder brother of Police drummer Stewart, had recently set up his own label, IRS Records. He was keen to get Sabbath on board, telling Iommi he had confidence in their ability to deliver, and so the band signed a deal that lasted for several albums. Perhaps seeing this as a new start, Iommi seemed determined to put together a strong line-up this time out, first engaging legendary drummer Cozy Powell. Despite rehearsals commencing with Tony Martin, Iommi was keen to get Ronnie James Dio back on vocals, a move that did not work out—he was still looking at other singers, but reportedly Powell persuaded him to stick with Martin. Geezer Butler was also thinking of returning, but he was ruled out as he had signed up to tour with Ozzy, promoting the latter's *No Rest for the Wicked* album. No permanent bass player was brought in before the album was recorded, but Laurence Cottle—better known in the jazz/rock world—provided the bass on the record as a session man (ex-Whitesnake and Colosseum II bassist Neil Murray was to join for the ensuing tour). The loyal Geoff Nicholls retained his full membership status, which was good to see. Martin wrote the lyrics this time out, taking the trademark Black Sabbath 'horror' imagery and basing the whole album around that theme. Recording took place in the autumn of 1988, with the release coming some months later in April 1989, and Iommi and Powell handled the production duties between them. The record was not a huge seller, making No. 31 in the UK, but only No. 115 in the US (although there were some distribution problems in North America apparently), but critically, the reviews were generally better than for any Sabbath album for years and it remains popular with fans.

In keeping with the title and theme of the album, the front cover featured a stark, black and white illustration of an old graveyard cross, designed by Kevin Wimlett. It was very atmospheric, to be sure, though it did seem odd at first glance that the cross shown was far from headless, in fact featuring a head very prominently. However, the back cover resolves this by showing the same cross with the head broken off and lying on the ground beside it. The album also came with an inner sleeve featuring the lyrics. Colour was added to the cover for some overseas releases.

Songs

'The Gates of Hell'
Another one of those short 'intro tracks', but it does at least make some sense as it opens the album. It does not do an awful lot in a musical sense, but it is appropriately scary-sounding, with atmospheric keyboards and what sounds like mysterious backward vocals coming together to get the listener into the right mood, and introduce the title song.

'Headless Cross'
Stepping away from the 'up-tempo opener' template for the first time in over a decade, this huge track is introduced by the big, echoey sound of Cozy Powell's drums before Iommi comes in with one of his very best, slow, monolithic, crushing riffs. In fact, two slow,

monolithic, crushing riffs—as the opening one gives way to another of equal bulldozing power heralding the verse. The vocal takes a full minute to come in, so measured and confident is the opening section, and when the chorus comes, it is stirring and huge, yet still creepy rather than triumphant. Tony Martin comes into his own here, developing a vocal presence that evokes both Dio and Ozzy by turns, when the music demands it, and it is clear how underrated he is in the Sabbath chronicles. Lyrically, this returns to the earliest Sabbath themes of pure horror film black magic as it tells the tale of how the titular cross was the scene of satanic meetings and sacrificial ceremonies, sealed by the flash of lightning that severed the head of the cross during the first of these such rituals. The song was released as a single, in slightly edited form, and there was a promo video made that featured the band performing (with Martin hamming it up enormously), intercut with the story being told via images of hooded monks, torches, candles, scroll, mist—you name it—and, of course, the lightning beheading the cross. It is over the top, but entertaining, and even Cottle appears on bass (he was absent from publicity photos of the time), though the camera studiously avoids him. All in all, this is an important track, recapturing the Sabbath spirit more successfully than had been done for some time. It remained a stage favourite throughout Martin's time with the band, and deservedly so.

'Devil & Daughter'

A more up-tempo track, but not in the 'too fast' vein that so often fails to suit Sabbath. In fact, the pacing of this (and the central riff itself) is more reminiscent of 'Children of the Grave' than anything else—that fast yet rolling tempo, which carries so much more power than mere speed. Martin puts in a great performance here, including an 'operatic metal' scream that really shows his range. The lyric is a simple one about the devil and his 'man-eater' daughter; it has been suggested that the song was in fact about Don Arden and Sharon, but this seems very unlikely since Martin was not even with the band during the Arden era. One thing about this album is that it is probably fairly safe to take the songs at their face value—Tony Martin approached this with a 'horror film' mentality, and it works just fine on that basis.

'When Death Calls'

Apart from the title song, this is the track from the record that stayed the longest in the live set, and it is easy to see why. This is magnificent. Opening with a slow, moody, menacing introduction, softly sung verses alternate with the massive rolling boulder of a chorus. The lyrics here are unassailably grim, with lines such as 'For I believe Satan lives, in the souls of the dying' causing a genuine chill. The song really takes off, however, on the three-and-a-half-minute mark when the pace picks up with a faster, bone-crushing riff, with Martin's delivery of the lines beginning 'Don't look, in those sunken eyes' perfect, and simultaneously catchy and scary as hell. In between the two verses of this section, the guitar solo is on this occasion provided by none other than Brian May of Queen, who shows with the way he peels off this blistering effort exactly where his true musical heart lies. The song returns to that huge chorus again, repeated for the last minute of the song and giving no room for breath. There is not a moment wasted in these seven minutes or so, and it is clear that this is the best Sabbath work since at least 'Heaven and Hell', and possibly even before. Tremendous stuff.

'Kill in the Spirit World'

A slightly lighter feel to this one, as the horror-story subject matter is somewhat incongruously accompanied by music sounding a little like 'Eye of the Tiger' by Survivor, with a dramatic chorus thrown in. It is not bad, but it is a little less substantial. What does save this one is Iommi's masterful guitar solo coming in at just after the second minute. Full of soul and emotion, it is no exaggeration to rank this among his very best solos. Overall, the song has slightly overstayed its welcome by the five-minute mark, but the solo makes you forgive it.

'Call of the Wild'

Another big-sounding, good-against-evil tale, resembling Dio's work very strongly both in Martin's vocal and the musical structure of the song. Cozy Powell's drums are also extremely powerful here. Allegedly, the track was originally to be called 'Hero', but was changed at the last minute owing to the fact that Ozzy had a song of that name on his album *No Rest for the Wicked*. It is hard to verify this claim either way, but it does make some sense as the track has, in an odd way, two choruses: one featuring the phrase 'Call of the Wild' very prominently but the other, and bigger chorus of the two, referring to that would-be titular 'Hero' in each line, including many repetitions toward the end. The same claim has been made about 'Devil and Daughter' being changed from the title 'Devil's Daughter' after that title was also featured on that same Ozzy album, but this is harder to believe given that the title 'Devil's Daughter' would make less sense with the lyric, wherein that phrase is never used.

'Black Moon'

A slight whiff of filler surrounds this track, which was originally recorded in a different key, in fact, as the B-side to the single version of the title track from *The Eternal Idol*. That is probably its level in truth as the music is a little throwaway and forgettable, while the lyrical imagery is starting to wear ever so slightly thin over the whole album. This time out, our 'hero' is finding himself summoned to Lucifer while the black moon rises, as he declares heaven to be 'no friend of mine', etc. It is good, Sabbath-y imagery for sure, but a whole album in that same vein becomes a little overdone by this time. Time for the six-and-a-half-minute final track to bring us back up to greatness?

'Nightwing'

A big, drama-laden 'quiet-loud' epic of sorts, developing into a faster and more powerful guitar riff just before the first solo, puts this above the previous two tracks and closes the album on something of a high. It has been claimed that the 'Nightwing' of the title is not some flying demon searching for souls and other victims, but in actual fact refers to an owl. Again, no verification for this, but it does make sense from the lyric. Iommi is busy meanwhile with no less than three, all accomplished solo spots here, and the album finishes strongly.

Related Song

'Cloak and Dagger'

Devils, screams, evil games, souls torn apart, the shadow of death, they are all here in this non-album track, originally used as the B-side to the 'Headless Cross' single. However, this surprisingly does not add up to another B-movie horror story recipe as this song is, on the face of it, about a woman who is playing her 'evil games'—more Evil Woman than Black Sabbath, if you like. However, it has been widely taken to actually be from the point of view of a man losing his faith in God. Whatever the lyrical inspiration, the track is a little lighter in tone musically than most of the album itself, and it was probably a good move to leave it off the original vinyl (it has since, of course, made the cut as a CD bonus track). Cutting a mid-paced, bluesy groove, along the lines of 'Heart Like a Wheel', it does kick up its heels a little more towards the end, but overall can be filed under 'inessential'.

15

Tyr

Release date: 20 August 1990
Record Label: IRS
Personnel: Tony Iommi, Tony Martin, Geoff Nicholls,
Cozy Powell, Neil Murray

When the band (now joined by Neil Murray on bass) convened at Rockfield Studios, Wales, in February 1990 to record the follow-up to *Headless Cross*, Tony Iommi had asked lyricist Martin to be a little more subtle with the words this time around, feeling that the constant satanic/horror imagery on the previous album had been a little bit too much, and he certainly got his wish as the singer arrived with a clutch of songs directly inspired by Norse mythology. As Iommi stated in his autobiography:

> On *Headless Cross*, Tony had just come into the band and he assumed, oh, Black Sabbath, it's all about the Devil, so his lyrics were full of the Devil and Satan. It was too much in your face. We told him to be a bit more subtle about it, so for *Tyr* he did all these lyrics about Nordic gods and whatnot. It took me a while to get my head around that!

In fact, this change of emphasis worked quite well because, although a new lyrical departure for the band, it was still full of the sort of often dark, epic imagery that suited the Sabbath brand, and in any case, it is not the theme for the entire album. Tyr is the name of the

Norse god of war and martial valour, and the album title is thus *Tyr* and not 'T.Y.R' as it is sometimes mistakenly credited. Recording took place throughout the first half of the year, with Iommi and Powell again handling the production duties, and when released, it reached a reasonably creditable No. 24 in the UK charts.

The front cover design of the album features a shot of a brooding, Scandinavian-looking sky, with the band's name above and the album title in runic letters below, accompanied by some nicely done Norse or slightly Gaelic-looking border work. The back cover features two similar sky views, in side-by-side panels, with the album title represented by a 'Tyr's hammer' logo in between, and the song titles in the respective panes. Although having no gatefold, the original vinyl did come with a nicely designed inner sleeve featuring the lyrics and some more of that nice Nordic artwork. The runic letters on the front are, in fact, not strictly correct, as the middle character, while resembling a letter 'Y', and thus used to spell the title, is actually the equivalent to the modern letter 'X' or 'Z', and so the title is not actually spelled 'Tyr' at all. Credited to the Design House 'Satori', the album artwork is regarded quite positively by many fans.

Songs

'Anno Mundi (The Vision)'

Now this is the way to open an album. Beginning with a short, quiet section, the band soon kick in with a classically epic-sounding groove that I would not even describe as a riff, as such—it is simply a big, loud, and proud widescreen backing to allow Tony Martin's vocals to really shine, soaring over the top of the music. Featuring some of the most intriguing and thought-provoking lyrics of his tenure with the band, the song appears to take as its jumping off point a rumination on the state of the world, but moves from there through a morass of metaphor and hidden meaning. *Anno Mundi* itself ('The Year of the World' in Latin) refers to a calendar based on time elapsed since Biblical accounts of the creation of the world. Most commonly, this is used by Jewish scholars and dates from 3,761 BC. By the end of the song, this fascinating lyrical subject matter has become inextricably linked with the music, and the lengthy coda possesses much of the majesty of something like 'Kashmir' or 'Stargazer'. A definite peak of the post-Ozzy era, this is one of the songs that illustrates just how undervalued this era of the band often is. No direct Norse material yet, of course—that would follow shortly.

Note: The subtitle 'The Vision' originally appeared in the lyrics as reproduced on the album's inner sleeve, but not on the outer cover track listing.

'The Law Maker'

A much more straightforward, fast, and heavy track here. With Powell driving the track along with a bass drum pattern bringing to mind Motörhead's 'Overkill' or 'Bomber', the song does what it intends to do, but is rather insubstantial in truth. Musically, it is one-dimensional, with the guitar solo fast and well-delivered, but oddly generic for Iommi, and the lyrics are weak. Telling the story of what amounts to a kind of supernatural bounty-hunter ('He's evil and mysterious' we are told, helpfully), lazily convoluted lines like the absurdly Yoda-esque 'The prince of darkness inside you will dwell' do it no favours at all. A weak link for sure.

'Jerusalem'

Now this is better again. A juddering, propulsive riff drives this song onward, while the chorus in particular imbues it with some more of that Rainbow-esque epic quality. Tracks like 'The Law Maker' and 'Trashed' have dated badly as they show the band aping the styles of their contemporaries and becoming influenced by those who, in turn, once took influence from the early Sabbath material, but this and similar tracks still shine as they show a band who wanted to remain one step ahead of the pack. They did not always manage that feat during this period, but when they made the effort, the difference was, and is, palpable. Lyrically, the biblical storyline could be said to be about Moses, leading the people to the Promised Land, or it may be a general warning about false teachers, but either way, it is a good lyric undermined by an incongruous opening. While the verses are packed with the likes of crying angels, 'walking in the valley' (of the shadow of death, presumably) and souls rising from the sea, the track opens with the somewhat bizarre and out-of-place 'The highway's screaming, callin' out your name'. Good track, though.

'The Sabbath Stones'

We are almost back in *Master of Reality* territory here, with this inexorably slow-paced, chugging behemoth of a song. Indeed, there is even a twice-repeated quiet interlude carrying the spirit of *Sabbath Bloody Sabbath* to complete the tip of the hat to 'classic Sabbath', and a vintage sped-up outro evoking the final section of the song 'Black Sabbath' itself. The lyric appears to lend weight to the theory of the previous track referencing the story of Moses as the titular 'Sabbath Stones' are clearly intended to be the Ten Commandments. In fact, while the album is not, as some have lazily painted it, a concept album with a Norse flavour, every song on here (with one notable exception coming up shortly) does appear to be about religion in some regard, which lends some much-appreciated gravitas to the whole aura of the record. Ian Gillan, for example, for all his fine qualities, was never a 'Sabbath lyricist'. Tony Martin, at this point, assuredly is.

'The Battle of Tyr'

Another one of those pesky keyboard instrumentals, this time opening up side two of the original vinyl, but really only serving as a harbinger of the Norse material and a minute-long introduction to the following track.

'Odin's Court'

Itself a bridge to usher in the mighty 'Valhalla' after it, this is nevertheless a beautifully sung, tastefully arranged song with some complementary and sensitive playing from Iommi to set against the wistful character of Martin's voice.

'Valhalla'

In a way, this could be seen as the concluding part of a three-track 'Norse suite' as it takes the themes opened in the last track to their obvious and grandiose conclusion. Fast-paced, yet still retaining the 'epic' feel of the best of the songs on here. The unashamed Norse Saga of the lyrics reaches chest-beating levels of grandeur during the chorus cries of 'Valhalla!', which induce in the listener the irrational desire to sing along lustily while taking to the oars of a longboat. This is the stuff.

'Feels Good to Me'

Completely out of step with the rest of the album both lyrically and musically, this big-hair, scenery-chewing power ballad was, by the band's own admission, simply included as an attempt to get a hit single. Thankfully the tactic failed because this song diminishes both the album and the Black Sabbath name completely. As a typical MTV-era rock ballad, it is serviceable enough, but it is even less fitting to Sabbath than 'No Stranger to Love' was, and at least that had the excuse of originally being intended for a solo album. Dropping this track into the middle of an otherwise conceptually 'epic' album was akin to dropping a meat pie into a large bowl of custard—even if you like the pie on its own, in the custard, it ruins everything. There was even a video produced for the song when it was released as a single, which was dreadful even by the standards of the time—all fast cars, bare-chested, lion-maned Adonises and hot girls on motorbikes. A chapter we shall draw a veil over, I think.

'Heaven in Black'

Back on track for the closing track on the album, we have a powerfully heavy mid-paced rocker following on from 'Valhalla' almost as if the track in between had never happened. The lyric clearly relates the legend of Postnik Yakovlev, the architect who designed St Basil's Cathedral for Ivan the Terrible, who proceeded to have him blinded so that he could never create anything as beautiful again for anyone else (try fitting lion-maned, bare-chested biker dudes into that for a video). The story is almost certainly apocryphal as there is evidence that Yakovlev continued to work after that date, but it is the kind of legend with religious overtones that suits the tone of the album perfectly. It is a strong way to finish off an album that, while perhaps not quite as strong overall as *Headless Cross*, certainly completed a trilogy of very high-quality albums in the 'Tony Martin era'. Sadly, for the next album, commercial rather than artistic agendas came into play and threatened to derail the band.

16

Dehumanizer

Release date: 22 June 1992
Record Label: IRS (UK), Reprise (US)
Personnel: Tony Iommi, Ronnie James Dio, Vinny Appice, Geezer
                Butler, Geoff Nicholls

Musically, the Tony Martin-fronted Sabbath had been making some
excellent strides and were arguably helping to restore some sense of
continuity to the Sabbath legacy again. However, after the *Tyr* tour
had finished, things began to get complicated once more. Firstly,
Geezer Butler, who had guested with the band and fitted in as well
as he ever had, indicated a wish to rejoin, which was endorsed by the
fair-minded Neil Murray. However, it got more complex when Ronnie
James Dio, who had also played with Geezer, came onto the scene and
began discussions with Iommi about a reunion. When it was agreed,
he suggested bringing in his then-current drummer, ex-AC/DC man
Simon Wright. This was rejected by Iommi and Butler, who wanted
to continue to use Cozy Powell. This in turn led to somewhat fraught
rehearsal sessions, as Powell and Dio had bad blood from their
Rainbow days and the atmosphere was reportedly extremely strained.
It was only inadvertently solved when Powell suffered a pelvic injury
in a horse-riding accident and Vinny Appice, drummer from the *Mob
Rules* days, stepped in. Things continued to get convoluted, however,
with Martin being asked back to cover while Dio went away for a few
days, and then being shown the revolving door again on his return.

Iommi has later described the band as being 'volatile' at the time and
has acknowledged that the chemistry was simply not there. There had
also been a conflict over song lyrics according to Iommi, who claims
in his autobiography that they had to specifically ask Dio to refrain
from his tendency to use fantasy imagery and, specifically, rainbows.
Unsurprisingly, however, the commercial pull of Dio's return was a
help, particularly in the US where it made No. 44, the band's highest
charting album for some time. In the UK, it more or less kept pace with
the previous two albums, reaching No. 28. The album was produced
this time out by Reinhold Mack, who had worked with ELO and
Queen. As an aside, notice also the slightly anomalous 'American'
spelling of the title. Quite some way from those four blokes from
Aston, one could say.

   The cover illustration by Wil Rees has come in for some criticism
over time, though it does depict the overall theme of the album. A
sort of 'Robot Grim Reaper', clutching a scythe and standing in
front of some sort of monitor screen, 'zaps' a long-haired youth
clad in jeans and T-shirt, apparently turning him into some sort of
machine in the process. The back cover design was simple, with the
tracks in an arched pattern over four monochrome band head shots,
though again the album did come with an inner sleeve, with the lyrics
reproduced.

Songs

'Computer God'

The theme of the album, and indeed the cover art, is encapsulated on
this opening track, with lyrics written by Geezer (according to Iommi)
about computers taking over and beginning to rob humans of their
humanity ('dehumanizing', in other words). It is an interesting concept,
and it tries to match it musically, but while it is heavy and satisfyingly
mid-paced (albeit with quiet section and uptempo conclusion), it lacks
something, both in terms of vocal melody, which is not up to Dio's best
standards, and also in the production, which leaves it feeling thin, and
with a particularly bright and trebly drum sound that kills off the depth
of the sound.

'After All (The Dead)'

Another crushingly heavy track, this one invokes the *Master of Reality* era with its down-tuned, gloomy tempo, and is unusual for a Dio-sung track in that it sounds as if it would have been perfectly matched for Ozzy. Normally, their respective songs sound like chalk and cheese, as the saying goes. Musing on the afterlife and what form it may take, the lyric is perfectly matched to Sabbath on this occasion. A big improvement on the opening track, it still struggles against those terribly produced drums which threaten to overwhelm the whole album, but it manages to rise above that and get away with it.

'TV Crimes'

On this track, we find Dio ploughing an unusual furrow lyrically (for him at least), as he takes on the subject of 'Televangelists'—that peculiarly American phenomenon of evangelists appearing on TV to relieve the faithful of their money, in varying degrees of honesty, shall we say. It is a sharp and well-written lyric, married to a fast accompaniment featuring some superb bass work from Butler. It does, once again, lack something in the melody department, though to refute that opinion it did make No. 33 in the UK charts when released as a single, so maybe some listeners found different. There was a video made of the track, which bizarrely ignored the subject matter entirely in favour of a tale about a stolen television. Opening with the TV in question being stolen at gunpoint from a Pawn Shop (the TV Crime, quite literally), it appears to be some kind of magic TV set as it works without any power as people carry it around and only ever plays Black Sabbath performing this song. After passing through the hands of several people, from homeless man to teenage rock fan, the set is eventually returned to the same shop it started in, where the lucky current owner manages to swap it, in somewhat unlikely fashion it has to be said, for a Gibson SG guitar in the window. Like the song itself, the video is fun, but certainly inessential.

'Letters from Earth'

Another satisfyingly trademark Sabbath chugging slow-paced riff opens this track very promisingly, though sadly it does not really build on that promise and struggles a little not to crumble under the weight of sustaining its four-plus minute running time. The lyrics are interesting, whereby the central character, despairing of the evil and violence around him, seeks to somehow rid the world of them in the form of the titular letters—possibly written to God, though this is not made clear. There was an alternate version of the track, featuring some different words and a slightly better production feel, which was used as the B-side to the TV Crimes single. There is a great instrumental section in this take as well, all of which lifts it above the album version. It is frustrating really because this could easily have panned out as classic Sabbath, but something, somehow, is missing; especially from the version used on the album.

'Master of Insanity'
This track was brought in by Butler, having been originally been recorded by his own Geezer Butler Band. Again, it is lyrically interesting, with the 'Master of Insanity' accused of being behind all of the world's tragedies, sins and woes. Who, though, is this character? It may be the old Master of Reality himself, Satan, but on the other hand, it may well be, like 'Heaven and Hell', a reference to the devil in all of us. Musically, however, this is lacking. The sometimes leaden playing married to another paucity of strong vocal melody mark this out as entirely disposable.

'Time Machine'
A very, very heavy track, this one seems to show the influence of Metallica, who were riding high at the time with their self-titled album (aka *The Black Album*), but without being in thrall to that influence. It is a hard, fast, anvil-heavy track with Dio lyrics about a metaphorical rather than literal time machine; it seems to deal with the way one can take control of one's life in the technological, computerised world which surrounds us. A definite stand-out on the record, it was actually first recorded some time earlier, in a different version, for use in the film *Wayne's World*, where it features fairly briefly in a scene with actor Robert Patrick parodying his T-1000 character from *Terminator 2*. The song is playing in Wayne's car as he is flagged down by Patrick (possibly as an in-joke, since the T-1000 character came back from the future in the *Terminator 2* film). This alternate version of the song, produced by Leif Mases, was later used as a bonus track on a CD reissue of the album.

'Sins of the Father'

Now, as is the frustrating pattern with this album, we are back to another unremarkable track after the triumph of 'Time Machine'. Beginning as a moderately interesting psychedelic Beatles-sounding track, with a vocal line straight from Ozzy's tenure, the song soon develops, unsurprisingly, into a rather generic up-tempo rocker with a paucity of interesting melody. The lyrics have some interesting ideas, with the song being open to interpretation about whether it refers to a victim of abuse, a wrongly convicted man or indeed a genuinely Biblical meaning, but the musical side of the track fails to give these ideas the opportunity to germinate. Another low on the back of a high point, unfortunately.

'Too Late'

Another excellent song here, as the rollercoaster ride of this album continues. A big, slow, semi-balladic dramatic piece telling the story of a man who has made a deal with the devil some time earlier only to find it is now time to pay and he is alone. With a truly impressive lyric, it is in places genuinely unsettling and one of the few places on this album where there is a let-up from the basic 'heavy' template. More light and shade like this would have helped the record immeasurably. Another contender for the highlight of an album that is quite probably the most wildly inconsistent the band ever recorded.

'I'

Once again, here we have a great song, as the album heads to a strong conclusion. Blessed with surely the shortest song title ever used, this paean to independence, ego, selfishness, or solipsism depending on the listener's viewpoint comes rampaging out of the speakers with an irresistible march of defiance. Perhaps slightly overstaying its welcome by the end, it is nevertheless a strong track, and Iommi's wah-wah drenched solo is a thing of perfection.

'Buried Alive'

They were so close to a great finish to the album. After two great tracks back to back, this one lets it down a little. Put simply, it sounds derivative. Death metal and grunge were two of the genres that had emerged to a large extent thanks to the unique flowering of Black

Sabbath back in the 1970s, but here were the masters seeming to try to ape the young pretenders. The chorus of this song is reasonably close to classic Dio, but the rest is just one big heavy ball of grunge metal, and it does not sit right at all. Indeed, Dio himself sounds totally out of place with it. Lyrically, it is again interesting because—as is usual with Dio—it is not literally about what the title may suggest, but instead appears to be looking at someone's indoctrination into an organised religion, and their subsequent reticence to admit to themselves when it fails to provide the answers they wanted.

Overall, this album has to be classed as a bit of a missed opportunity. The 'dream team' were back together, but it was an uneasy alliance, and the fractured sound of the album reflects this. Big seller or not, the suspicion remains that this was a misstep, and that the developing Tony Martin Sabbath identity should have been allowed to grow organically. After this line-up collapsed in on itself during the subsequent tour, Martin was back again. Yet impetus had been lost, and the end of the chapter would not be too far away.

17

Cross Purposes

Release date: 31 January 1994
Record Label: IRS
Personnel: Tony Iommi, Tony Martin, Geezer Butler, Bobby
                Rondinelli, Geoff Nicholls

As the *Dehumanizer* tour rumbled on, some inter-band relations were becoming strained, and this came to a head when the band agreed to support Ozzy's band at a couple of shows at Costa Mesa, California, where a reunion of sorts had been discussed. Dio flatly refused to perform these dates, describing Osbourne as a 'clown', and he was effectively out of the band. Sabbath went ahead with the contracted shows, with Judas Priest singer Rob Halford stepping into the breach and, with very little rehearsal time, handling the vocals adeptly on both nights. Vinny Appice also departed, and rehearsals for the next record saw ex-Rainbow drummer Bobby Rondinelli (post-Dio Rainbow, we must add) being drafted in along with the return of the ever-dependable Tony Martin. Geezer Butler stuck around for this album, but departed before the next. Produced by Leif Mases, who of course had worked with the band on the *Wayne's World* version of the song 'Time Machine', the album's commercial reception sadly showed up the power of a 'brand' since it failed to get close to the success of *Dehumanizer*, reaching No. 41 in the UK and a disappointing No. 122 in the US.

   The front cover art for the album is a rather impressive picture of an angel with burning wings, although in a similar way to the 'baby photo' that became the *Born Again* cover, it seems no one at the time realised that the same image was used as the basis for the cover to the Scorpions' single 'Send Me an Angel' three years earlier. This has been addressed down the years, and it seems that it was indeed a genuine oversight. That apart, the Sabbath usage of the image is the far superior cover, and it remains one of their more striking designs to this day. The rear cover simply has the track listing with some flames, so nothing to get excited about there, unfortunately. At this time, vinyl was becoming very much the poor relation to CD, and unsurprisingly, there was again no gatefold, though the album did come with an inner sleeve having the lyrics on one side and full credits on the other. For most vinyl copies, the 'burning angel' image is fairly small in relation to the cover dimensions, making this a rare example of the CD looking more impressive as it took up nearly the whole of the CD front cover. Some copies of the vinyl did have the image in larger scale, however.

Songs

'I Witness'

A good, up-tempo, yet not out of place song to open the album, a driving riff underpins this whole track, propelling it on to its conclusion. Not a Sabbath classic, but a good opener certainly. The lyrics, telling obliquely about someone heading to a new start of sorts, are full of paradoxical wordplay, such as 'the hounds of heaven' and 'a darkness which illuminates you'. It is also notable for the use of the word 'Sabbocracy'—make of that what you will.

'Cross of Thorns'

The first real classic on this album comes along here, with this beautifully textured, atmospheric piece moving from quiet passages to big, heavy riffing, and a massive instrumental section in the middle to set it off. Slightly odd fade-out, however, with the unaccompanied voice of Martin left alone by the music, and fading despairingly into the ether. The lyrics are loaded with religious imagery, and indeed this, together with the reference to '400 years', could well mark this out as being inspired by the Troubles in Northern Ireland, as the 400 years would correlate roughly with the first English occupation of the country. Thought-provoking, with some real depth, it is a great song, proving again how underrated and overlooked the Martin-era albums were, and still are.

'Psychophobia'

A lesser track here, as this short, three-minute song is fast and furious, but with a lack of melody and an uninspired riff. Lacking any of the trademark Sabbath sound, this is a disappointment after the strong start the album had. Again, the lyrics are interesting, possibly taking inspiration from a religious cult leader, but their impact is fatally blunted by the unsympathetic arrangement.

'Virtual Death'

This one was, according to Iommi's autobiography, a collaboration musically between him and Butler, and he describes it as 'a heavy, powerful riff' that he was pleased with. He is right in regard to the fact that there are moments in this track that conjure the spirit of classic early-1970s Sabbath like few things since (an instrumental section around halfway through the song in particular could, like so much of this era's material, have fitted seamlessly onto *Master of Reality*). Truth is, the whole song could easily have been sung by Ozzy; in fact, he would be more effective than Martin on this, to these ears. However, overall, the track is unsatisfying—the bassline carries too much of the song at the expense of the guitar, leaving it too plodding and one-dimensional, and providing a palpable sense of relief when that trademark grinding guitar makes a real appearance. The lyrics appear to be referencing the protagonist being in a state of some misery by unspecified parties who have wronged him, which he describes as 'virtual death', and are serviceable at best. Ultimately, this is a frustrating song as it could have been so much more.

'Immaculate Deception'

Once again, here we see the '70s Sabbath atmosphere brought to life, as Iommi creates a twisting, descending riff that could easily have graced one of the first four albums. This leads into a fast-paced chorus that complements it well, with a more contemporary sound. A frenzied guitar solo over a frantic-paced backing sets the seal on a very effective track, which sees the central character drawn under the spell of the darker side of this world, and loving it. A good end to the original first side of vinyl.

'Dying for Love'

A real change of pace here, with this big, lighter-waving ballad dealing with righteous revolution and standing up to oppression (it has been suggested that this was directly inspired by the situation in the former Yugoslavia at that time). Whatever the source of the subject matter, it is a perfect marriage of the music and the sentiment of the song, with Martin excelling in his delivery. Where this differs from vintage Sabbath songs dealing with Butler's love of peaceful revolution (such as 'Children of the Grave') is that this is upfront in its message, without being couched in any metaphorical imagery. Not better, or for that matter worse, but different, and just as valid as any of those old classics. Excellent stuff, indeed, if atypical for any Sabbath line-up including Iommi, Butler, and Martin.

'Back to Eden'

Here we have the exact opposite to the previous track, with a similar message about searching for peace this time hung on a sci-fi framework, with the song opening with 'the star demons' offering, or threatening, to bring the human race 'back to Eden' once they are tired of endless 'Freedom fighting Freedom'. It is quite an entertaining track, if a quite commercial sounding one, and bereft of the earnest nature of 'Dying for Love'. Not great, but not bad.

'The Hand That Rocks the Cradle'

Another collaboration between Iommi and Butler, according to the former's autobiography, and, once again, a pretty decent effort. Lyrically, there could be several inspirations behind this, all of which have been put forward at one time or another. Taken at face value, it could be referring to a real-life case of a woman imprisoned for serial infanticide, or slightly less literally could be about abortion doctors and whether they are taking infant lives or not. Taking it still further from the realm of the literal, it could even be metaphorically about one's dreams being crushed and stymied without them having a chance to grow. Whatever the truth of this—and it could well be a mix of all three, or more, meanings—the balladic intro to the song makes it appear as it is going to be another 'Dying for Love' until Iommi comes in with a riff that owes much to some of Jimmy Page's work with Led Zeppelin, which then proceeds to anchor most of the rest of the track, in quite hypnotically, effectively repetitive manner (though an instrumental outburst breaks up proceedings). Once again, quite un-Sabbath-like, and one might not be able to pick Black Sabbath out of a line-up, if you like, but it is pretty good. There was a promo video made for the song, but it is not a great work to be frank—shot in arty black-and-white, it is all mood shots of a young girl superimposed over film of the band playing and does not advance the cause of the song much if at all.

'Cardinal Sin'
A very topical song this time, firmly rooted in the real world, which is, according to Iommi, written about a Catholic priest in Ireland who hid his love child for over twenty years. Of course, with more recent news stories concerning similar ecclesiastical individuals, the song could also be extrapolated to encompass other areas of covert sin and hypocrisy. Musically, it is certainly strong, with a shuddering, staccato riff doing the heavy lifting before giving way to more up-tempo passages driving it along. It has been reported that the song was originally to be titled 'Sin Cardinal Sin', with the shorter title being adopted only after a printing error omitted the first word from the sleeve, but this cannot be verified.

'Evil Eye'
Finishing off the album is this mid-tempo grinding rocker, which is sadly unexceptional both in terms of musical ideas (not many beyond the riff) and the lyrics, which are the standard 'evil woman' template that Sabbath have used periodically since album number one. Some nice solo action going on here, but that is all that really elevates the track. The most interesting thing about this one is the Eddie Van Halen connection. Eddie is thanked in the credits, and the story is that he actually came up with the riff along with Iommi, but that business reasons prevented his receiving the songwriting credit he should have had. Rumours have also persisted over the years that he also played on the track; specifically, the second guitar solo. However, in his

book, Iommi refutes this—while admitting that he met up with the band while Van Halen were playing in Birmingham, he claims that although they jammed on the song, he failed to properly record the solo that Eddie Van Halen played, and the opportunity was wasted.

Related Song

'What's the Use?'

For some unaccountable reason, the Japanese release of *Cross Purposes* contained an extra track compared to the rest of the world: namely this breathlessly paced track that appears as the final song on this particular release. It is not essential, having as much of a feel of Iron Maiden as it does Black Sabbath, but it is certainly a good enough track to blow the cobwebs away when in the mood for this sort of thing. It actually bookends the album better than 'Evil Eye', so the question of why it was denied to the rest of the world is a somewhat puzzling one, but in a way one which sums up this almost-great, but ultimately slightly lacking album.

The impression left by this record is that, after the hasty scrambling of the *Mob Rules* line-up again for the slightly ill-advised *Dehumanizer*, the momentum built up over the previous three Tony Martin releases was lost. Certainly, this does not sound like the work of such a focused unit as those responsible for *Headless Cross* or *Tyr*, which is a real shame as those albums represented the organic growth of a genuine 'third Sabbath' after the Ozzy and Dio eras. For all of the problems that could be found in this album, however, they were as nothing compared with what was to come up next.

18

Forbidden

Release date: 20 June 1995
Record Label: IRS
Personnel: Tony Iommi, Tony Martin, Neil Murray, Cozy Powell,
                Geoff Nicholls

When the *Cross Purposes* tour came to an end, Bobby Rondinelli departed and Bill Ward came back in on a temporary basis to do a few dates in South America, which planted the first seeds of a reunion of the original foursome. After these dates, however, Butler left again to rejoin Ozzy's band in an ongoing 'soap opera' kind of situation. Iommi got Neil Murray and Cozy Powell back in again, meaning that it was the *Tyr* band that got together in 1994 to start writing and rehearsing for this album in Wales, before recording commenced at Parr Street Studios, Liverpool, in the December of that year. The record company had what they regarded as a brainwave when they suggested getting guitarist Ernie C from the metal/punk/rap band Body Count to produce the album, in order to bolster what they saw as the flagging 'street cred' of Sabbath. As part of their masterplan, they also suggested drafting in Ice-T, hip-hop/metal artist and Body Count singer, to contribute some vocals to one track. Iommi says in his autobiography that he 'reluctantly' went along with this, but that none of the band were happy, especially Powell, and he described the album bluntly as 'crap' and the production as 'awful'. When the album emerged, it received criticism from fans and press alike, and even in the UK, it only managed to limp to No. 71. Is it really as bad as its reputation suggests, however?

Another element of the album to come in for some flak was the cartoon cover of the grim reaper, while wrapping around to the back it turns out to be waiting by flames emerging from an open grave, containing terrible cartoon images of the band members' heads (including Ice-T and Ernie C). In truth, it has a certain 'EC horror comics' charm to it, but the lack of a gatefold on the vinyl does destroy the wraparound picture idea, in much the same way as Deep Purple's *Stormbringer* and ELP's debut also did. Still, CD was taking over by this time anyway, so it is hardly surprising that little effort went into the vinyl edition. The artwork was done by cartoonist Paul Sample, best known for his long-running biker-themed comic strip Ogri and a series of book covers, including some for Tom Sharpe.

Songs

'The Illusion of Power'
The track featuring a spoken verse by the aforementioned Ice-T, this actually starts with a very promising and atmospheric introduction before getting dragged down immediately when the main riff emerges. The verses are half-spoken by Tony Martin, who sounds a little like a fish out of water with the whole thing as he struggles to glean some melody where there really is none. The chorus is a little better, and Ice-T's brief verse is well enough done if hopelessly out of place. It is no wonder that this opener put people off the album as soon as they listened to it because it really does not bode well.

'Get a Grip'
A much better song here as it happens. Not a classic, of course, but it is propelled along by an uber-heavy churning riff, rolling casually along like a steamroller down a slight hill, inexorably and satisfyingly crushing everything in its way. Things take a turn for the worse in the messy chorus, not to mention a dreadful 'shouty' section at the end, but overall, it is pretty good. The drum sound is terrible, sounding as if Powell is banging on suitcases, but that is a pattern throughout the whole album as producer Ernie C just could not seem to 'get' heavy

rock drums. The lyrics are rather dull fare, unfortunately, ruminating on how dreadful things are in the world in a vague kind of way, while encouraging us all to 'get a grip'. A partial success, then.

'Can't Get Close Enough'

Now this is better still. A nice, gentle, melodic introduction leads into a sprightly riff not dissimilar to 'Megalomania', which can only be a good thing. It gives way to the reflective section again to close the song. It could be longer, and more substantial, for sure, but what is here is extremely good. Even the lyrics provoke a little thought again as it is interesting to speculate whether the unknown subject of the song, who is always 'too far away', is in fact God or some sort of divine power. This interpretation would certainly fit the lyric, and at this point, any open-ended interpretation is a good thing, particularly after the previous tired lyrical exercise. Excellent song, keeping the album so far on track.

'Shaking Off the Chains'

The album hits a new low with this dirge-like and lyrically dull effort. Once again, and badly so this time, the matter of 'melody' appears to have been bypassed entirely, with Martin simply reduced to bellowing against the artless riffery. It improves a little when it speeds up to an up-tempo section, but only by comparison. By any normal Sabbath standards, it is still crashingly dull. The lyrics may be about someone stuck in an unidentified dead-end life or they may be addressing addiction—the sad truth is that the way they are delivered it is hard to care. One from the very bottom shelf of Sabbath deliveries without a doubt, sad to say.

'I Won't Cry for You'

A little better again here, as this schizoid album attempts to raise its head above the water again. Kind of in the 'big rock ballad' vein once again, this tale of someone suffering the consequences of their own making and thus deserving no sympathy is delivered with a certain sense of dynamics and feeling as a powerful riff in the chorus and some of Iommi's very best soloing on the album raise this to the position of possibly the best song thus far, closing the original vinyl side one.

'Guilty as Hell'

Rather average again here, as a cocksure, strutting riff attempts to drive a song that really does not have much going for it. Bitter, vitriolic lyrics cannot save this one, as we see once more that, sadly, behind the 'velvet curtain' of the competent riffing, there is really very little to see. The vocal melody is once again desperately weak, putting the seal on this one.

'Sick and Tired'

The perfect example here of extremely workmanlike material that is just about saved by a heroic Iommi performance. The song itself is, once again, poorly thought out, with the lyrics, again full of spitting bitterness, failing to convince as Martin sounds as if he really is not all that bothered. No, what saves this slight, three-and-a-half-minute effort is Iommi's soloing contribution, scattering salvos of lead guitar work all over the track like sparks in a welding studio. Certainly, were it not for this, the song would be deemed a complete failure. As it is, it is only half a failure, but the album needs a big finish to save it.

'Rusty Angels'

Here comes the start of that much-needed big finish. The best track here by some way, this is the only song on the album that can legitimately be described as a genuine Sabbath classic. Every element is in place here, from the subtle opening section through the spring-heeled riff (with echoes of Rush at their finest) driving the song along to the arpeggiated chorus that carries such a typically Sabbath feel to it that it is easy to imagine Ozzy at his best delivering it. Add on a storming Iommi solo playing the song out and suddenly it is easy, and also frustrating, to see just how good this album could have been. The only negative is again the terrible drum sound, but that can be overlooked. Martin's lyric about a hard-hearted woman who is as ugly inside as she is beautiful outside, and who needs to let some love, or faith, into her heart before it is too late, is very good, and for one of the few times on this album, it is accompanied by a really top-class vocal melody. A track to restore one's faith in this incarnation of the band, and to show that they could still punch their weight when they set their minds to it.

'Forbidden'

Not quite up to 'Rusty Angels', but still the strong close to the album continues with this excellent title track. A powerful, heavy Iommi riff propels the song, but does not dominate, as Martin's commanding vocals and Nicholls' keyboards are prominent here. Managing to be both heavy and also big, melodic, and almost commercial, it is another fine cut. One starts to wonder whether much of the hate for this album comes from people forming a strong negative opinion from the earlier tracks, and it being too late to win them back.

'Kiss of Death'

The album proper closes on this fairly lengthy note, as 'Kiss of Death' goes through several distinct sections over the course of its six minute duration. One part of the song, around three-quarters of the way through, is especially noteworthy for containing a riff that sounds as if it could even have been a left-over from the first four Sabbath albums—it has so much of that earthy power and doomy gravitas. With lyrics that sound as if they could be referencing the mysterious woman from 'Rusty Angels' yet again, it is a great finish to an album, which, had it been re-sequenced, produced better, and perhaps just had a little more time taken in the writing stage, could have been regarded as a respected farewell for this era of the band. As it is, it suffers with a greatly undeserved reputation as, in many eyes, the worst Sabbath album, which is not the case at all. It is, to these ears, probably stronger than *The Seventh Star* or *Born Again*, and at its strongest, it is easily the equal of *Eternal Idol* and maybe also *Cross Purposes* and *Dehumanizer*.

Related Song

'Loser Gets It All'

As with 'What's the Use' on the previous album, the Japanese release once again got an extra song added to the end of the album. However, whereas that particular track strengthened the end of the album considerably, this one does not. It is not a bad song, and indeed is pleasant enough in a throwaway, poppy-metal sort of way, but after the great finish to the main album, this comes over as very much of an anti-climax. Mind you, it could easily have replaced one of the weaker tracks earlier in the running order, such as 'Shaking Off the Chains' or perhaps 'Guilty As Hell', and arguably improved things overall.

After the subsequent tour to promote the album, the band fell apart, and the reunion of the original line-up was not far away. Apart from a couple of tracks added to the *Reunion* live album, and three more for the compilation *The Dio Years*, there were to be no new Sabbath studio recordings for almost two decades until three of the original foursome finally made their way with some purpose into the studio once again. The critical and fan reaction to *Forbidden*, plus the drum production that marred one of Cozy Powell's last major albums before his untimely death in 1998, still leave something of a pall over the way the Tony Martin era ended, which is something of a pity as there is much great music left as a legacy there.

19

13

Release date: 10 June 2013 (UK), 11 June 2013 (US)
Record Label: Vertigo
Personnel: Tony Iommi, Ozzy Osbourne, Geezer Butler
                 (Plus Brad Wilk)

During the eighteen years separating this album from direct predecessor *Forbidden*, things had become rather convoluted in the Sabbath camp. The original foursome had reunited in 1998, releasing the *Reunion* live album, before going on hiatus again a few years later. Having never officially disbanded, when the *Mob Rules* line-up reformed again in 2006, they had to perform under the name Heaven and Hell. Their album, *The Devil You Know*, was released under that name and is thus outside the direct scope of this book, enjoyable as it was. Following Dio's death in 2010, they disbanded and the Black Sabbath name was resurrected again, although without Bill Ward, who failed to agree terms with the other three original members. Therefore, it was that Rage Against the Machine drummer Brad Wilk came to handle drum duties on this album, although Tommy Clufetos was the choice for live work.

After the initial announcement of the reunion at a press conference in November 2011 (still featuring Ward at that time), Tony Iommi was diagnosed with lymphoma, the shocking news of which was released in January 2012. As a result of his need for ongoing treatment, and the difficulty of travel, rehearsals and recording for the album were switched from the planned California location to Iommi's home in Warwickshire, England. After Ward's final failure to agree terms in May, work commenced in August 2012, by which time several songs had been written, with recording being completed in the following January. The album was produced by Rick Rubin, prolific record producer and engineer and co-founder of Def Jam Records; Rubin had been lined up to handle production duties when the original foursome had begun recording an abortive album in 2001. Released to a fanfare of publicity and greater widespread interest than at any time since the early '70s, the album reached No. 1 in both the UK (where it was the band's first chart-topping album since *Paranoid*) and in the US, which seems somewhat surprising given the pitiful sales figures of the Tony Martin-era albums over there. Such are the vagaries of public interest.

For the album cover, designers Nick Dart and Neil Bowen of Zip Design hired sculptor Spencer Jenkins to build an 8-foot-tall wicker model of the number '13' in a field in Buckinghamshire, which was then set on fire and photographed by Jonathan Knowles for the cover image. The resulting conflagration was reportedly dramatic and enormous, and visible for miles. When put together with the Ward/Wilks/Clufetos/Appice soap opera, and the odd Heaven and Hell band name episode, the whole gestation and realisation of this album could only have been more Spinal Tap had one of the drummers perished in a 'bizarre gardening accident'. The panoramic view of this massive fiery title continued around the back of the cover of the CD release, with the song titles also on the back cover, while the double-vinyl release had an impressive landscape shot of the blaze spread across the inner gatefold. Nothing like going out with a bang.

Songs

'End of the Beginning'
Right from the start of this eight-minute opener, the similarity to the self-titled 'Black Sabbath' track from the very first album is evident. A slow, boulder-rolling-downhill opening hammer chord sequence gives way to single note verses in exactly the same way as that earlier song before an up-tempo section arrives compounding the resemblance.

This clearly has to be a nod back, and the song takes on its own identity from then on. Ozzy is on surprisingly good form when one considers widespread reports of the vocal problems he had displayed in live performances for quite some time. Indeed, he sounds better here than at any time since the first three or so of his solo albums in the early '80s. Iommi's solos rewind the clock back to his superlative work on *Technical Ecstasy*, while Geezer Butler announces his return as lyricist with a thoughtful lyric that he says was inspired by the potential of cloning in our technological near-future ('robot ghosts' as he memorably phrases it in the lyric), while also clearly sending a message on another level to be an individual and not a blind follower in society. With all of the elements in play here, it was as if they had never been away. The song was actually premiered during the finale of season thirteen of the TV show *CSI*, an episode in which the band made a guest appearance, and was also used in the end credits of the Seth Rogen comedy film *This Is the End*. The track was released as the second single from the album.

'God Is Dead?'
This track, another eight-minute-plus affair, was the first song premiered, being released as a taster for the album as the first single and also as a free download for those who pre-ordered the full album via iTunes. With a lyric based on the writings of Friedrich Nietzsche (who famously said 'God is dead. God remains dead. And we have killed him. How shall we comfort ourselves, the murderers of all murderers?'), the song powerfully depicts someone struggling with his own morality, conscience, faith, and place in the world. Again, musically, this is a slow-paced and very heavy piece, albeit with some effective light and shade and a trademark up-tempo section to provide contrast. The track has quite strong echoes of *Volume 4*, and with its memorable chorus, it is easy to see why it was the first song showcased. The sleeve of the single reinforces the Nietzsche connection, illustrating the man himself against the backdrop of an atomic bomb detonating. Ozzy seems less comfortable with some parts of this song, but still acquits himself well overall. The track was featured in the promo for the sixth season of the TV show *Sons of Anarchy*, about a rebel motorcycle club, and was also awarded the Grammy for Best Metal Performance in January 2014.

'Loner'

The third and final single from the album, this five-minute track is a much more direct piece of work. Driven by a main riff that drives along in irresistible fashion, causing the listener's foot to tap unstoppably, it is broken up by quieter vocal sections in similar fashion to much of the *Sabbath Bloody Sabbath* material, along with a secondary riff to keep things from getting too repetitive. Ozzy is clearly relishing the delivery of the lyric here, which tells of an individual locked inside his own non-communicative world and issuing a warning about the dangers of this self-imposed isolation, and this is felt in the almost joyous vocal delivery. A live version of the track, recorded at its first ever public performance, was also released by the band as a 'single' via their YouTube channel. A perfect song to stop the slight fear of the album adhering too much to the template set by the first two songs.

'Zeitgeist'

A real change of pace here, with this reverb-drenched acoustic piece a clear nod to 'Planet Caravan'—hand drum accompaniment and all. It follows that track in its lyrical content as well, with space travel imagery throughout, though this time the meaning is much more obscure. The title (literally 'Time Ghost' in German) refers to the prevailing idea or spirit of a particular time, and it is hard to see how this marries up with the lyrical tale of a doomed space traveller adrift in his craft. It may be that the traveller is a metaphor for the idea itself, travelling through space and time to reach fruition, or indeed it may be a deeper reflection on life itself. Whichever way, it is a classically thoughtful Butler lyric. Musically, the similarity to 'Planet Caravan' is a little too close for comfort, and the track is no classic partly due to this, but it is a nice change of pace in a way that the albums from *Heaven and Hell* onward rarely employed.

'Age of Reason'

Back to the heavy material here, with Iommi's rolling, crushing riff powering this track along its seven-minute length. Butler returns to familiar lyrical themes here, with the song's ruminations on the state of the world (as ever, bad) and our attempts to improve it (as you would expect, doomed). Always good to know how we stand—

namely, helplessly. This has of course been a lyrical stock in trade of his dating back to the likes of 'Electric Funeral', 'War Pigs', and 'Children of the Grave', and it is good to see it back. References to 'Sustainable extinction', 'Jaded revolution', and 'Prozac days' leave us in no doubt of the message being delivered here. Meanwhile, musically, the song becomes more dramatic as it progresses, with a classic Iommi solo leading into a massive coda, and once again the classic spirit of Sabbath is captured like lightning in a bottle.

'Live Forever'

A sub-five-minute track here, and a simpler one both lyrically and musically. The lyric has the protagonist facing the end of his life and pondering his conscience. Clearly conflicted, he repeats over and over that he does not want to live forever, but he does not want to die. Musically, the song is probably the most direct and up-tempo on the record, careering along in relentless fashion. A slower pre-chorus gives a change of pace, but it is always back to that driving, repetitive jackhammer of a riff. It is not the greatest song on the album by any stretch, but as a straight-ahead rocker, it does its job well enough, preparing us for the remaining two lengthier pieces that close out the album.

'Damaged Soul'

Echoes once again of the very first Sabbath album here, as old themes of Satan and evil resurface in a lyric about a character possessed by evil, or at least believing he is, seeing the doom of humanity coming and accepting his own hopeless destiny to end in the clutches of Satan. It is unusual for Butler to return to this sort of theme, which he has not touched since those very early days, but of course that is one of the things contributing to this album's air of a farewell 'wrapping-up' of the band's career, which it does so well. Adding to that debut album feel, Ozzy even contributes harmonica on this track, as he did on 'The Wizard', and Iommi breaks up the graveyard-paced riff for some meandering soloing similar to that in 'Warning'. One could almost look at this song as being like a celebration of that long-ago debut in microcosm, and it does it so in such style that it even manages to cause some quite emotional nostalgia in the process. I do not think anyone was expecting this.

'Dear Father'

The album ends on a harrowing note here, with this tale of a man abused by a priest as a young boy, having his life and faith irrevocably damaged as a result, and finally tracking down his molester and murdering him in turn, asking him how he will face his God after his life of hypocritical sin. It is a powerful and sadly familiar tale, brilliantly delivered by Ozzy in his most sinister and unsettling vocal performance since the early '70s, and musically, the accompaniment is equally effective, with funereal-paced riff giving way to harmonically dramatic verses and brutally heavy faster parts. As a final, overt nod to the past, the song ends with the same rain and tolling bell that opened that very first album. An almost unbearably poignant ending to an album that quite superbly manages to summon up the real spirit of what Sabbath were all about, and which in many people's minds they were always about at heart, despite the excellence of some of the Dio and Martin albums. As a consequence of this, a slight shadow is cast over the album by the absence of Bill Ward. Make no mistake, Wilk does an excellent job throughout the album and no criticism should be aimed at his playing, but this really was the swansong that should have come from the original foursome. Whatever the reasons that prevented this from being a possibility, it remains a great shame. That said, however, we should still celebrate the album as an epitaph to the band's career, which few fans ever thought they would get—certainly not of this quality. It is a fitting way for them to sign off.

Related Songs

'Methademic'

The first of three bonus tracks on the Deluxe Edition of the album, this starts deceptively with around forty seconds of quietly picked acoustic guitar before a fast riff kicks the song in with a vengeance. Hard and heavy, it is nevertheless clear to see why it was only included as a bonus track as it is a little too one-dimensional and simplistic by comparison with the material on the album proper. Lyrically, it is also straightforward, being a condemnation of the use of crystal meth or methamphetamine. Nevertheless, having said that, it is an infectious riff and as a bonus song it is pretty good.

'Peace of Mind'

Quite short at under four minutes, this second bonus track is something of a tricky one to assess. On the positive side, it has an absolutely archetypal Sabbath riff, which could easily have graced *Master of Reality* without a second thought. However, on the other side of the coin, the vocal melody is lacking and it comes across a little as a classic riff in search of a song. Upping the tempo towards the end does not really add very much, and it is ultimately slightly frustrating that such a great riff could not have been incorporated into a more complete song. A nice lyric, though, concerning a man tormented by the mistakes he has made and how the world sees him, which could have probably been better served by a more thoughtful and melodic delivery. Partly excellent, but a bit of a waste of potential in the end.

'Pariah'

The third and final of these 'deluxe' bonus tracks, the Christian imagery employed here appears to be a message not to worship your idols and make them more than they are, be they rock stars or whoever. It is a decent enough, if quite harshly written, lyric, whereas musically it is just okay. Like the two tracks before it, a good infectious riff is ill served by the song, which feels almost like an afterthought bolted on top. They were ultimately correct to leave these three tracks as the icing on the cake, rather than a part of the cake itself.

'Naïveté in Black'

Included alongside the three 'regular' bonus tracks on a 'Best Buy' special edition of the album, the most interesting thing to immediately jump out about this track is the title, which is clearly a play on the supposed meaning of 'N.I.B.', 'Nativity In Black', which the band have always denied. So, a cheeky in-joke then, for sure, but beyond that there seems to be little reasoning behind the title. There is certainly no reference to 'N.I.B.' in the lyric nor even naïveté in any obvious form. In fact, it is a straightforward plea to live one's own life and not interfere in others—maybe that could be seen as a naïve hope, but that is something of a stretch. Musically, however, it is very good and a shame it was not more widely released. Barrelling along unstoppably on a real machine-gun riff from Iommi, it is an absolutely top drawer hard rocker to finish on. A criticism could be that it sounds a little more like an Ozzy Osbourne solo track *circa Bark at the Moon* (especially in the vocal melody department), but that would be a harsh thing to level at an honest to goodness cracker of a heavy rock song because sometimes, when all of the shouting is done, that is really all you need.

20

Live Albums

Perhaps surprisingly, given their reputation as a live act throughout their career, Black Sabbath have not been served as generously as one might expect in terms of official live albums. Along the way, though, there have been some real moments to savour. Here is a rundown of what is on offer (bootleg releases are available, of course, but are not covered here).

Live at Last (NEMS, 1980)

Track Listing: 'Tomorrow's Dream'/'Sweet Leaf'/'Killing Yourself to Live'/'Cornucopia'/'Snowblind'/'Children of the Grave'/'War Pigs'/'Wicked World'/'Paranoid'

Released in July 1980, *Live at Last* was, however, recorded some seven years earlier, in Manchester and London in 1973. It was released without the consent of the band—which by this time featured Ronnie James Dio—supposedly at the insistence of former manager Patrick Meehan. Very much a low-budget and cheap-seeming affair, the original cover (designed by Dave Field) featured an incongruous shot of a satellite above a lunar landscape, accompanied by the title in that ubiquitous 'computer font' of the time. It is difficult to see the relevance of this in any shape or form to the material within, and there was no gatefold or inner sleeve providing any further details beyond track listing and band line-up (and even that managed a—barely legible—typo in crediting Ozzy as 'Ossie'). However, such was the appetite for live Sabbath at the time that the album still managed to reach No. 5 on the UK charts.

In truth, while it shows the band on excellent form, the sound quality was not the best, and the choice of material for a single vinyl album baffling, with almost nineteen minutes being taken up by a sprawling rendition of 'Wicked World'. The version of 'Killing Yourself to Live' here—the only track from that year's *Sabbath Bloody Sabbath*—is interesting as it is a formative version with different lyrics. The fifty-three-minute running time did not help the sound on vinyl as it pushed the limits of a single album, especially a heavy rock record. The album was later remastered and released officially as the first half of a double album *Past Lives* in much better form.

Live Evil (Vertigo, 1982)

Track Listing: 'E5150'/'Neon Knights'/'N.I.B.'/'Children of the Sea'/'Voodoo'/'Black Sabbath'/'War Pigs'/'Iron Man'/'The Mob Rules'/'Heaven and Hell'/'The Sign of the Southern Cross'/'Paranoid'/'Children of the Grave'

This double live album, recorded during the *Mob Rules* tour and released in December 1982, was (according to Iommi) prompted by the releases of both *Live at Last* and also the Ozzy Osbourne live album *Speak of the Devil*, which consisted entirely of old Sabbath songs. Lasting eighty-three minutes, and therefore slightly too long for a single CD, the original CD issue of the album omitted 'War Pigs', while the subsequent remastered edition restored this but cut out much of the stage announcements and banter from Dio. It has since been issued as a double CD with all of the original track listing present. It is a good collection, and well recorded and played, though Dio does struggle on some of the older material—particularly 'Black Sabbath' and 'Children of the Grave'—which was so closely associated with Ozzy. The Dio-era material is well performed, though 'Heaven and Hell' is dragged out interminably and tests even the strongest patience. The album cover is interesting in that its illustration includes visual depictions of every song on the album—including the closing excerpt from 'Fluff', which is represented by an acoustic guitar washed up on the shore on the back cover. Interestingly, while the album charted both in the UK and the US, it did not score anything like as highly in the UK as the sloppily-released *Live at Last* had done.

The band fell apart somewhat acrimoniously during the mixing of the album, amid tales of Dio sneaking into the studio to remix his vocals louder—something he has always denied. Iommi has spoken of Dio as assuming a more controlling manner in the band at the time, and his own separate solo contract did not go down well with his bandmates. Iommi and Butler eventually finished the mix themselves after the departure of both Dio and Appice. Perhaps tellingly, Appice (along with Geoff Nicholls) is not listed as a full member, but only under 'Special Thanks'.

Cross Purposes Live (IRS, 1995)

Track Listing: 'Time Machine'/'Children of the Grave'/'I Witness'/'Into the Void'/'Black Sabbath'/'Psychophobia'/'The Wizard'/'Cross of Thorns'/'Symptom of the Universe'/'Headless Cross'/'Paranoid'/'Iron Man'/'Sabbath Bloody Sabbath'

Released in 1995, this album, recorded unsurprisingly on the *Cross Purposes* tour at Hammersmith in April 1994, was originally released as a CD/video set, but has been unavailable for some years. In truth, this is a shame as the album is a very good performance and surely ripe for a reissue. The presence of Geezer Butler alongside his old sparring partner Iommi gives the sound a rock-solid anchor, and Tony Martin and Bobby Rondinelli both acquit themselves well. Of particular note is some of the lesser-performed material, which is revisited here, such as 'Symptom of the Universe' and 'Sabbath Bloody Sabbath', both complete with their original codas, which were not generally performed live with Ozzy. It is a high-energy performance that has dated well.

Reunion (Epic, 1998)

Track Listing: 'War Pigs'/'Behind the Wall of Sleep'/'N.I.B.'/'Fairies Wear Boots'/'Electric Funeral'/'Sweet Leaf'/'Spiral Architect'/'Into the Void'/'Snowblind'/'Sabbath Bloody Sabbath'/'Lord of this World'/'Dirty Women'/'Black Sabbath'/'Iron Man'/'Children of the Grave'/'Paranoid'/'Psycho Man'/'Selling My Soul'

History was made in December 1997 when the original Sabbath foursome reunited once more, initially for two homecoming concerts at Birmingham's NEC Arena, from which this live album comes. The final two tracks on the album are new studio recordings (see below).

The sound on the album, courtesy of veteran producer Thom Panunzio, who had worked extensively with Ozzy on his solo material, is quite astonishing. The tracks fairly leap from the speakers, and the overall effect is so 'live' sounding that it is almost as if the band were appearing in your living room. Added to this, the adrenalin and joy of being back together clearly gives the whole band a rush, and they are on top form. Some tracks here, such as 'Spiral Architect', 'Behind the Wall of Sleep', and 'Lord of this World', were completely unexpected, as was 'Sabbath Bloody Sabbath', though the latter is shorn of its closing section. The album cover, designed by Glen Wexler, depicts two goat-legged and winged demon children holding a shield aloft emblazoned with the band name, in the form of a coat of arms, while the rear has the track listing shown above a crowd shot.

Studio Tracks

Both of the new songs included here are credited to Osbourne and Iommi only, with Ozzy writing the lyrics on this occasion. This is the only time in the history of the band where any songs have been credited to these two alone. Both tracks were recorded in April–May 1998, and were produced by Bob Marlette.

'Psycho Man'

A fairly straightforward lyric for this one (as stated, unusually written by Ozzy) about a serial killer, but all the more effective with the music in a way precisely because of its directness. The song is driven by two fine Iommi riffs, the first half bludgeoned along by a slow, menacing, and anvil-heavy power-riff, with the second part a bit more up-tempo and taking the track to an exciting conclusion, as if the titular character is stepping up his killing spree. A prime Iommi guitar solo adds the icing on the cake for a song that is perhaps not a classic, but certainly far from being the throwaway that many would expect for a 'bonus song' that was apparently created rather quickly in the studio. A worthy addition to the canon.

'Selling My Soul'

A shorter song here, and a little less substantial than 'Psycho Man', it is nevertheless a strong track. The lyric deals with a man who has either literally or metaphorically sold his soul, and is married to a powerful riff with more than an echo of Leslie West's work with 'Mountain'. Unlike 'Psycho Man', this track does not feature Bill Ward; apparently his drum track was deemed not to be sufficiently in time, so a drum machine was used for the final release. This is serviceable enough, but it does seem sad that Ward was replaced on the second of the final two studio tracks released while he was in the band.

A couple of years after these tracks appeared, the band did go into the studio with the intention of recording a full album, but the sessions did not work out in the end. One track, called 'Scary Dreams' was even played live several times, supposedly to preview the release of the album which never was. It would be interesting to say the least to hear those sessions, as it was reported that none of the material ended up on the *13* album a decade later.

Past Lives (Sanctuary, 2002)

Track Listing: Disc 1: As per *Live at Last*.
Disc 2: 'Hand of Doom'/'Hole in the Sky'/'Symptom of the Universe'/'Megalomania'/'Iron Man'/'Black Sabbath'/'N.I.B.'/'Behind the Wall of Sleep'/'Fairies Wear Boots'

A superb release here, which puts the original *Live at Last* material into a fitting setting and context finally. The original album occupies Disc 1 of this double CD set, while Disc 2 contains three tracks recorded in 1975 on the *Sabotage* tour, along with some excellent material from 1970, sweeping up the early tracks which were missed off the hodgepodge that constituted *Live at Last* the first time around. In this context, and with the *Live at Last* material given a sonic makeover, which improves it considerably, this can be considered as definitive a Sabbath live document as we have. Adding in excellent packaging and extensive new liner notes makes this essential.

Live at the Hammersmith Odeon (Rhino, 2007)

Track Listing: 'E5150'/'Neon Knights'/'N.I.B.'/'Children of the Sea'/'Country Girl'/'Black Sabbath'/'War Pigs'/'Slipping Away'/'Iron Man'/'The Mob Rules'/'Heaven and Hell'/'Paranoid'/'Voodoo'/'Children of the Grave'

Released as a limited edition of 5,000 copies, this album—recorded over three nights between 31 December 1981 and 2 January 1982—obviously overlaps considerably with *Live Evil*. The exceptions to that being the appearances of the songs 'Country Girl' and 'Slipping Away', it can still be seen as a rather strange release given the paucity of official live Sabbath material. The original limited release sold out quickly, but the album was later included on a second CD with the 2010 deluxe edition of *Mob Rules*. The original album contained a replica programme, the front cover of which also provides the album cover, but it should be noted that this programme was actually from the January 1981 UK dates of a year earlier than the recording, which constituted the latter leg of the *Heaven and Hell* tour after Appice had replaced Ward.

   The band did seem to have something of a fascination with the Hammersmith Odeon, since as well as this album and *Cross Purposes Live* both being recorded there, the deluxe edition of *The Seventh Star* also contained a show recorded at the same venue, this time with Ray Gillen on vocals, from *The Seventh Star* tour. That particular offering was far less noteworthy, however, and really did show the band at possibly its lowest ever ebb.

21

DVD and Video

Much like the live album situation, video material officially released of the band has been surprisingly slim pickings over the years. There have been a few releases of note, however, and we take a look at them here.

Note: I have not included documentary videos, of which there have been a few.

Never Say Die (1978)

Track Listing: 'Supertzar'/'Symptom of the Universe'/'War Pigs'/'Snowblind'/'Never Say Die'/'Black Sabbath'/'Dirty Women'/'Rock and Roll Doctor'/'Electric Funeral'/'Children of the Grave'/'Paranoid'

Perhaps the best example of the excitement of a Black Sabbath show captured on film, this recording of a Hammersmith (where else!) show on the 1978 tenth-anniversary tour may have captured a band that was in the process of falling apart, but this would never be apparent from the performance captured. It is almost all solid gold from beginning to end, with the intro music of 'Supertzar' almost sending shivers down the spine on its own, proving the track to have met its perfect function as it builds the suspense until the band crash into a devastating 'Symptom of the Universe'. The inclusion of 'Rock and Roll Doctor' may raise a few eyebrows, but other than this, there are no missteps here, with 'Black Sabbath' and 'Dirty Women' being particularly powerful before the one-two of 'Children of the Grave' and 'Paranoid' provides a stunning conclusion. In fact, the only disappointment of this release is what it fails to include: the show was edited down to sixty minutes for the original VHS tape release, this being the standard length of music videotape releases at the time. This necessitated the removal of 'Iron Man' and 'Fairies Wear Boots' (both originally placed directly after 'Electric Funeral' in the set list), as well as chunks of guitar and drum solos and some instrumental work. Even when released on DVD years later, this footage has never been reintroduced into the show, leading to questions about whether the original master tapes still exist. Nevertheless, what is included here is magnificent.

Black and Blue (1981)

Track Listing (split between Black Sabbath and Blue Öyster Cult): 'The Marshall Plan' (BÖC)/'War Pigs'/'Neon Knights'/'N.I.B.'/'Doctor Music' (BÖC)/'Cities on Flame' (BÖC)/'Divine Wind' (BÖC)/'Iron Man'/'Paranoid'/'Godzilla' (BÖC)/'Roadhouse Blues' (BÖC)/'Heaven and Hell'/'Born to be Wild' (BÖC)/'Die Young'

This oddity of a release came from a co-headline tour of the US in 1980 by Black Sabbath and Blue Öyster Cult, known as the *Black and Blue* tour, with an October show at Nassau Coliseum being filmed. The resulting concert film was first released to cinemas before appearing on VHS videotape shortly after. The film itself is an odd mishmash of songs by the two bands, scattered together rather than one band after the other. This was presumably done to encourage fans of both bands to stay for the whole show in the cinema, but it makes for rather unbalanced viewing. It also, of necessity, omitted a large proportion of the set from both bands, making it a compromise offering at best, though the performances are decent throughout (although it must be said, they are hampered by some very poor filming, with camera angles being extremely haphazard). The release has never come out on DVD (though it did appear on Laserdisc during the short lifespan of that particular format). Reports from various sources including distributors indicate that this is largely because they Sabbath camp have opposed its release.

The Last Supper (Sony, 1999)

Track Listing: 'War Pigs'/'N.I.B.'/'Electric Funeral'/'Fairies Wear Boots'/'Into the Void'/'Sweet Leaf'/'Snowblind'/'After Forever'/'Dirty Women'/'Black Sabbath'/'Iron Man'/'Children of the Grave'/'Paranoid'

Filmed during the 1999 tour by the reunited original band, this DVD almost certainly holds the distinction of 'most frustrating Black Sabbath video release' even among the catalogue of missed opportunities they have had. The performance here is absolutely excellent, and the choice of material is pretty good as well, but bizarrely, and unforgivably, the editors decided to break up almost every song by interview segments with the band dropped randomly in the middle of the tracks. Even more ridiculously, when the original video was replaced by the DVD release, it was left exactly the same instead of the obvious solution of having the concert and the interviews as two separate features, or even an option to view with or without the talk. As it is, this makes for such an infuriating viewing experience as to make what should have been a superb show virtually unwatchable. We can only hope this shambles can be remedied on a subsequent release.

Live… Gathered in Their Masses (Vertigo, 2013)

Track Listing: 'War Pigs'/'Into the Void'/'Loner'/'Snowblind'/'Black Sabbath'/'Behind the Wall of Sleep'/'N.I.B.'/'Methademic'/'Fairies Wear Boots'/'Symptom of the Universe' (instrumental)/'Iron Man'/'End of the Beginning'/'Children of the Grave'/'God Is Dead?'/'Paranoid'
Bonus tracks in deluxe set: 'Under the Sun'/'Dirty Women'/'Electric Funeral'

A superbly filmed DVD here from two shows in Melbourne, Australia, with the band displaying their impressive stage show,

lights, back projections, etc. Iommi and Butler roll back the years
spectacularly, playing and looking as good as they ever did, and even
Tommy Clufetos does a great job behind the drum kit, helping to
soften the blow of Bill Ward's absence. Ozzy has suffered the most
over the years, physically and vocally, but while he is undeniably a
shadow of the imperious stage figure he was back in the 1970s, he
still makes this more genuinely and authentically 'Sabbath' than any
other vocalist could do. There have been claims that the vocals have
been 'cleaned up' in some places when comparing this to raw footage
from other sources, but such is to miss the point. This is a celebration
of the greatest heavy metal band ever, and there would be no place
for excessively off-key vocals to spoil that, even if such was the case.
This should be enjoyed for what it is. It is not up to the *Never Say
Die* DVD musically, but it is far better visually, and these two releases
together make up the best live Sabbath we are going to experience on
the small screen for now—at least until the *Last Supper* footage gets
properly edited at any rate.

22

Compilations

Unsurprisingly, there have been a host of Sabbath compilations over the years, particularly in more recent times, and to list them all fully would be futile. I will go through a selection of the most significant ones, however.

We Sold Our Soul for Rock 'n' Roll (NEMS, 1975)

Track Listing: 'Black Sabbath'/'The Wizard'/'Warning'/'War Pigs'/'Iron Man'/'Paranoid'/'Wicked World'/'Tomorrow's Dream'/'Fairies Wear Boots'/'Changes'/'Sweet Leaf'/'Children of the Grave'/'Sabbath Bloody Sabbath'/'Am I Going Insane'/'Laguna Sunrise'/'Snowblind'/'N.I.B.'

The first Sabbath compilation to come out, this was something of a masterstroke in the UK as it included the track 'Wicked World', which had only appeared on the US release of the debut album. In those days, long before 'bonus tracks' or even availability or knowledge of import releases, many fans did not even know of the existence of this track, and thousands of copies of this double album were undoubtedly sold to people just wanting to get hold of that one song. It does seem strange, though, that 'Evil Woman' was not included as that could have repeated the trick for the US market who had missed that song on the original album. There are some selection oddities

('Changes' and 'Laguna Sunrise', plus the full 'Warning' seem odd, as is 'Am I Going Insane' being the sole representative of *Sabotage*), but it was a desirable item back then, even if it was released without the band even knowing about it. The packaging was striking, with the lettering in red on black, with the 'S' letters being rendered as white 'lightning bolts', while the inner gatefold cheerily pictured a young woman in an open coffin, with original pressings also including a four-page booklet of band photos, in a similar way to the original *Volume 4* release. A significant release, as many fans' introduction to the band.

Greatest Hits (NEMS, 1977)

Track Listing: 'Paranoid'/'N.I.B.'/'Changes'/'Sabbath Bloody Sabbath'/'Iron Man'/'Black Sabbath'/'War Pigs'/'Laguna Sunrise'/'Tomorrow's Dream'/'Sweet Leaf'

The only other compilation to appear during the original band's time, this was a somewhat baffling release. Basically, the *We Sold Our Soul for Rock 'n' Roll* album cut down to a single album, it was left as a comparatively lengthy single vinyl record, leading to slightly inferior sound as well as missing key tracks from the double album. Also, the title '*Greatest Hits*' seems a little inappropriate for a band who had only had one hit single up to this point. A somewhat puzzling release, though it was packaged in a sleeve featuring a rather splendid, and appropriately gloomy, Breughel painting 'The Triumph of Death'—although even this was spoiled by wrapping it around a non-gatefold sleeve. All in all, notable, if strange...

The Sabbath Stones (IRS, 1996)

Track Listing: 'Headless Cross'/'When Death Calls'/'Devil & Daughter'/'The Sabbath Stones'/'The Battle of Tyr'/'Odin's Court'/'Valhalla'/'TV Crimes'/'Virtual Death'/'Evil Eye'/'Kiss of Death'/'Guilty as Hell'/'Loser Gets It All'/'Disturbing the Priest'/'Heart Like a Wheel'/'The Shining'

This compilation, which sneaked out fairly quietly in 1996 (it did not even have a US release), is an interesting one in that it steers clear of the well-worn furrows and instead mines the seam of the more overlooked albums from *Born Again* to *Forbidden*. Since many of these releases were somewhat patchy, this presents rather a good way to dip a metaphorical toe into the water of that phase of the band's career, and a good many people would probably be surprised at the quality of some of what they found. The big hitters from the period are present and correct here, including 'Headless Cross', 'When Death Calls', 'The Shining', 'Valhalla', and the title track. There are some glaring omissions, however—representing *Forbidden* without 'Rusty Angels' is unforgivable, while the inclusion of the throwaway bonus track from that album, 'Loser Takes It All', is completely baffling. Also, representing *Dehumanizer* with the sole track 'TV Crimes' hardly seems adequate. While the scope of the compilation creditably takes in all of the albums covered in the time frame, licensing issues mean that the non-IRS albums are represented by only a single track each: that is *Born Again*, *The Seventh Star*, and *The Eternal Idol*. These are also shunted to the back of the otherwise chronological track list, which makes the flow a somewhat butchered affair. Still, as a sweep-up of a rather fallow period, it is a decent enough representation, and with its arresting cover (band logo in the classic purple on back, with the title on an ancient-looking scroll) and a potted band history in the (rather thin) booklet, it is nice to have.

The Ultimate Collection (BMG, 2016)

Track Listing: 'Paranoid'/'Never Say Die'/'Iron Man'/'Black Sabbath'/'Children of the Grave'/'Fairies Wear Boots'/'Changes'/'Rat Salad'/'Sweet Leaf'/'War Pigs'/'Sabbath Bloody Sabbath'/'Hole in the Sky'/'Symptom of the Universe'/'Spiral Architect'/'Rock 'n' Roll Doctor'/'Dirty Women'/'Evil Woman'/'A Hard Road'/'Lord of this World'/'Into the Void'/'Behind the Wall of Sleep'/'Snowblind'/'Tomorrow's Dream'/'N.I.B.'/'Electric Funeral'/'Embryo'/'Killing Yourself to Live'/'Am I Going Insane'/'Wicked World'/'It's Alright'

Spread over a huge eight sides of vinyl, this 2016 release gets a noteworthy mention here not due to its content, which we will come to, but rather its astonishing packaging. It also came out on CD, but the vinyl release is the real deal here, with the cover unfolding into a giant crucifix, with one side depicting a dramatic flame-shrouded cross and the other having full-panel pictures of the four original members from their heyday, plus the front and back covers, with the front sporting a splendid 'demon/world in flames' image that was used in the promotion of 'The End' tour. It is the kind of thing that gets collectors salivating, and deservedly so. The content is, of course, hardly the point for this deluxe release, but for the double CD version, it is more likely to sell to the more casual fan. As such, it has great material as one would expect, but some astonishingly puzzling selections among them. For instance, the inclusion of 'Rat Salad' seems beyond reason, and selecting 'Embryo' without even having it in its rightful position before 'Children of the Grave' even more so. Similarly, 'Rock 'n' Roll Doctor', 'Am I Going Insane', 'Evil Woman', and 'It's Alright' would not be most people's selections of choice. Room really should have been made for 'Supernaut', 'Under the Sun', 'Megalomania', 'Gypsy', and 'Junior's Eyes', to name a few. Still, the vinyl behemoth is quite probably the most desirable Black Sabbath artefact yet released for the completist collector, and as such, it is a worthy headstone to commemorate the end of this legendary band's career—assuming, of course, it is the end.

Select Bibliography

Books

Gillan, I., *Ian Gillan: The Autobiography* (Music Press Books, 2016)

Iommi, T., *Iron Man* (Simon & Schuster, 2011)

McIver, J, *What Evil Lurks: The Complete History of Black Sabbath* (Race Point Publishing, 2016)

Osbourne, O., *I Am Ozzy* (Grand Central Publishing, 2009)

Tangye, D. and Wright, G., *How Black Was Our Sabbath* (Sidgwick & Jackson, 2004)

Wall, M., *Black Sabbath: Symptom of the Universe* (St Martin's Press, 2015)

Journals, Newspapers, and Articles

Alexander, P., 'Black Sabbath – Artist Guide' in *Mojo*, June 2014

Brannegan, P., 'This Is The End' in *Metal Hammer*, November 2015

McIver, J., 'The Story Behind Paranoid' in *Metal Hammer*, June 2010

Wright, J., 'Black Sabbath At The End' in *Goldmine Magazine*, July 2016